Bulletin Boards
for
Every Month

Bulletin Boards for Every Month

Jeanne Cheyney
Arnold Cheyney

Scott, Foresman and Company
Glenview, Illinois   London

Good Year Books

are available for preschool through grade 8 and for every basic curriculum subject plus many enrichment areas. For more Good Year Books, contact your local bookseller or educational dealer. For a complete catalog with information about other Good Year Books, please write:

Good Year Books
Scott, Foresman and Company
1900 East Lake Avenue
Glenview, Illinois 60025

5 6 MCG 95 94 93

ISBN 0-673-38828-X

Contents

PROJECT PATTERNS

Introduction

Bulletin Boards for Every Month is a book designed for teachers in the primary grades, although other elementary school teachers will undoubtedly find it useful. Every bulletin board illustrated in the book has patterns to go with it.

Here are some suggestions for making all your bulletin boards successful:

1. Solid-colored cloth works well as background material because it can be washed and used over and over again. If you use light-colored cloth and find that your bulletin board items don't show up well against it, try outlining the items with a broad-tipped marker.
2. Don't let yourself be limited by the bulletin board frame. You can extend figures and other items well beyond the bulletin board borders and onto the surrounding wall.
3. You can use any blank wall as a display surface.
4. Scotch Magic™ Tape adheres well to painted walls and is invisible on your wall display items.
5. Avoid washed-out looking bulletin boards by directing students to *press heavily* on their crayons when decorating display items.
6. Change your bulletin boards frequently to suit your classroom purposes.
7. Don't feel limited by what you see in this book. You can create terrific bulletin boards by mixing the patterns into original arrangements. All are interchangeable.
8. Enjoy!

Borders

Materials and Supplies

any paper or cloth—e.g., construction paper, typing paper, wrapping paper, wallpaper,
   newspaper (or painted newspaper), grocery bags, table paper, shelf paper, or felt
scissors
broad-tipped marker (optional, for outlining edges)

Small Bulletin Board Letters

Materials and Supplies

any paper—e.g., construction paper, typing paper, wrapping paper, wallpaper, newspaper
   (or painted newspaper), grocery bags, table paper, shelf paper
scissors

Large Bulletin Board Letters

Materials and Supplies

any paper—e.g., construction paper, typing paper, wrapping paper, wallpaper, newspaper (or painted newspaper), grocery bags, table paper, shelf paper

scissors

Materials and Supplies

light-blue background
dark-blue border and letters
gray paper (optional)
white paper
soda can
popsicle sticks
foil
candy and gum wrappers

small paper sack
Styrofoam cup
straw
crayons
scissors
broad-tipped black marker
cloth or wallpaper (optional)

Instructions

1. Discuss the problem of litter.
2. Prepare the trash can from the pattern on page 78, using gray paper.
3. Prepare the figures from the patterns on pages 75–78. Press heavily on crayons to color the figures, or dress the figures in cloth or wallpaper.
4. Prepare the trash; use wrappers, etc.
5. Outline all the items in black marker.

September

Materials and Supplies

light-blue background
dark-blue border and letters
white paper

colored paper—yellow, dark blue,
   brown, red, black, green, purple,
   and orange
scissors
broad-tipped colored markers

Instructions

1. Discuss colors.
2. Prepare the figures from the patterns on page 76. Cut one figure from each of the eight colors.
3. Make 3x7-inch labels from white paper. Use the broad-tipped markers to print colored letters on the labels.
4. Outline all the items in dark-blue marker.

Materials and Supplies

yellow background
black border and letters
white or manila paper
colored paper—red, green, and
   black

wide black bias tape (optional)
crayons
scissors
broad-tipped black marker

Instructions

1. Discuss safety.
2. Prepare the big figures from the pattern on page 75. Press heavily on crayons to color.
3. Prepare the traffic light from the pattern on page 79, using black, red, and green paper.
4. Make the lines from black bias tape or black paper.
5. Outline the figures in black marker.

September

Materials and Supplies

yellow background
blue border and letters
white or manila paper
crayons

scissors
glue
broad-tipped black marker

Instructions

1. Talk about people in the community who help.
2. Prepare the figures from the patterns on pages 75–76. Color heavily and add tools as needed. Outline with marker.
3. Prepare the tree trunk from the pattern on page 74. Color heavily black or brown.
4. Prepare the doll from the pattern on page 104. Color.
5. Prepare the puppy from the pattern on page 98. Color heavily.
6. Extend extra figures beyond the bulletin board, onto the wall, on all sides.

Materials and Supplies

light-green background
dark-green border and letters
manila or white paper
crayons
scissors

lined paper (optional)
broad-tipped black and green
  markers
cloth or wallpaper (optional)

Instructions

1. Have the children draw pictures of their families and write about them. Or they can just write their names.
2. Prepare the figures from the patterns on pages 75–78. Color heavily or dress as paper dolls with cloth or wallpaper (optional). Outline in black marker.
3. Add lined or white papers. Outline in green marker.

September

Materials and Supplies

light-blue background
black border and letters
colored paper—three shades of
  green (or white paper colored
  three shades of green), black,
  red, purple, yellow, and orange

scissors
glue
colored magazine pages (optional)

Instructions

1. Discuss harvest.
2. Prepare the trees from the patterns on page 74, using the black and various green papers.
3. Prepare the small fruits from the patterns on page 76, using the yellow, purple, red, and orange papers (or cut the shapes from colored magazine pages). Glue the fruits to the trees.

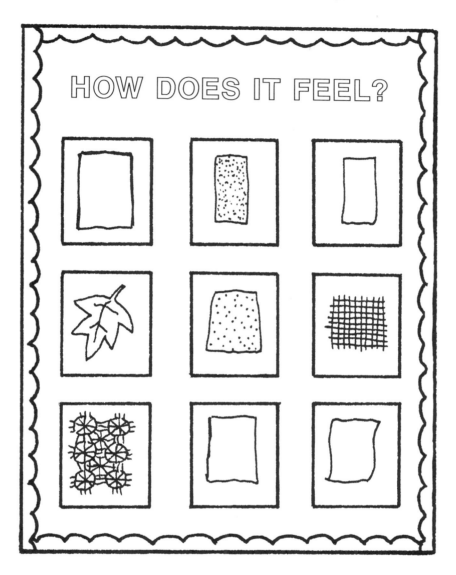

Materials and Supplies

dark-green background
white border and letters
items for touching
white paper

scissors
glue
Scotch Magic™ Tape

Instructions

1. Let the children feel the various items. Discuss the items. Use as many descriptive words as possible.
2. Glue or tape the items to white paper rectangles.

September

Materials and Supplies

dark-blue background
light-blue border and letters
manila, brown, or white paper
crayons

scissors
broad-tipped dark-blue marker
dark-blue paper (optional)

Instructions

1. Read about and discuss rest and sleep.
2. Prepare the sleeping face from the pattern on page 106, using brown, manila, or white paper. Color heavily.
3. Make four 4 x 24-inch labels from white paper. Cut dark-blue letters or print the words on the labels with a broad-tipped marker.

HARVEST

Materials and Supplies

large black letters
green, black, or brown construction
   paper
newspapers or grocery bags
   (optional)

green, black, or brown tempera
   paint (optional)
red, yellow, and purple paper
scissors
glue
Scotch Magic™ Tape

Instructions

1. Read about and discuss harvests.
2. Prepare the tree trunks from the pattern on page 80, using black or brown paper (or painted bags or newspaper).
3. Prepare the crowns by gluing together sheets of green paper (use various shades) or painted bags or newspaper. Make a 36-inch square, and then shape and cut. Glue the crowns to the trunks.
4. Prepare the big fruit from the patterns on page 79, using red, yellow, and purple paper. Glue to the crowns.
5. Tape the trees to the wall. Place loose fruit under the trees.

October

Materials and Supplies

black background
white border and letters
thin dinner-size paper plates
orange and black tempera paints
white or lined paper

orange paper in strips
scissors
crayons
broad-tipped orange marker

Instructions

1. Discuss fears, and have the children write about or draw pictures of things that make them feel afraid. Outline their papers in orange marker.
2. Prepare the pumpkins, using paper plates painted orange. Let the plates dry and then paint black features.
3. Prepare the ghosts from the patterns on page 81 or 82, using white paper. Color heavy black eyes and mouths.
4. Add the orange paper connecting strips.

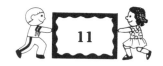

Materials and Supplies

light-blue background
black border and letters
white paper
colored paper—dark-blue and black

scissors
crayons
glue
broad-tipped black marker

Instructions

1. Read about and discuss Columbus.
2. Prepare the figure from the pattern on page 76, using white paper. Color heavily.
3. Prepare the ship from the pattern on page 83, using black paper except for white sails.
4. Prepare the waves from the pattern on page x, using dark-blue and white paper.
5. Outline the sails, waves, and Columbus in black marker.

October

Materials and Supplies

yellow background
orange border and letters
manila or white paper
small grocery bags cut to desired
   size
crayons
scissors

glue
Scotch Magic™ Tape
candy
broad-tipped black marker
dress materials (optional)

Instructions

1. Discuss good manners.
2. Prepare the figures from the patterns on pages 75–78. Dress with cloth as paper dolls, or color heavily with crayons. Outline in marker.
3. Attach candy treats with tape. Glue the bags to the figures' hands.
4. Prepare the balloons (size optional) for the figures' dialogue. Use the black marker to print the words and to outline the balloons.

Materials and Supplies

light-blue background
black border and letters
colored paper—red, orange, yellow,
    brown, and black

scissors
glue

Instructions

1. Discuss how leaves change, things to do with autumn leaves, and ways to have fun with fallen leaves.
2. Prepare the tree trunks from the pattern on page 74, using black paper.
3. Prepare the tree crowns from the pattern on page 74, using one red, one brown, two orange, and two yellow sheets of paper. Glue the crowns to the trunks.
4. Prepare small leaves from the pattern on page 82, using red, orange, yellow, and brown paper. The number of leaves is optional.

October

Materials and Supplies

yellow background
black border and letters
white paper
colored paper—black
thin dinner-size paper plates
orange and black tempera paints

small grocery bags
string
crayons
scissors
glue
broad-tipped black marker

Instructions

1. Discuss the concepts of "up" and "down."
2. Prepare the tree trunks from the patterns on pages 74 and 81, using black paper.
3. Prepare the ghosts from the pattern on page 81, using white paper. Color the eyes and mouths heavily in black. Outline the ghosts in marker.
4. Make the pumpkins by cutting the rims off paper plates and painting the centers orange. Paint black features or add features cut from black paper.
5. Make the owls from small grocery bags. Add yellow eyes, beaks, and feet, black eyes, and brown feathers. Color heavily. Tie the feet with string.

6. Make a moon by outlining a whole paper plate in black marker.

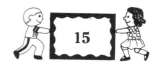

Materials and Supplies

yellow background
black and orange border
black letters
white paper
thin dinner-size paper plates

small paper sacks
orange and black tempera paints
string
crayons
broad-tipped black marker

Instructions

1. Talk about the concepts of "singular" and "plural."
2. Make the pumpkins by cutting the rims from paper plates and painting the centers orange. Add features with black tempera paint.
3. Prepare the ghosts from the pattern on page 81, using white paper. Color the eyes and mouths heavily in black. Outline the ghosts in marker.
4. Make the owls from small grocery bags. Add yellow eyes, beaks, and feet, black eyes, and brown feathers. Color heavily. Tie the feet with string.

Materials and Supplies

black letters
newspapers (optional)
white paper
colored paper—yellow and black
crayons
scissors
thin dinner-size paper plates

grocery bags
glue
broad-tipped black marker
string
lined writing paper (optional)
black and orange tempera paints
Scotch Magic™ Tape

Instructions

1. Discuss Halloween, and have the children write about or draw pictures of what they think Halloween is.
2. Prepare the tree trunks from the pattern on page 91, using black paper or newspaper painted black.
3. Prepare the branches from the pattern on page 92, using black paper or newspaper painted black.
4. Make a moon by cutting a 14-inch square from yellow paper and shaping. Outline the moon in black marker.
5. Prepare the ghosts from the pattern on page 82, using white paper. Color black eyes and mouths heavily. Outline the ghosts in black marker.
6. Make the pumpkins by painting paper plates orange. Allow to dry and then use black paint to add features. Outline the pumpkins in black marker.
7. Make the owls from small grocery bags. Add yellow eyes, beaks, and feet, black eyes, and brown feathers. Color heavily. Tie the feet with string.
8. Use tape to attach all parts of the display to the wall.

Materials and Supplies

light-blue background
black border and letters
manila or white paper
colored paper—black and light-
  brown
scissors

crayons
newspaper or grocery bag
  (optional)
black tempera paint (optional)
cotton (optional)

Instructions

1. Talk about Thanksgiving.
2. Prepare the trees from the patterns on pages 74 and 81, using black paper (or a grocery bag or newspaper painted black).
3. Prepare the houses from the pattern on page 85, using light-brown paper (or a grocery bag). Color the thatch roof yellow. Color the door and window heavily in black. Color the chimney red.
4. Prepare the table from the pattern on page 84, using light-brown paper (or a grocery bag). Cut and glue. Add wood-grain lines.
5. Prepare the figures from the patterns on pages 75–78, using manila or white paper. Color heavily.
6. Prepare the clouds from the pattern on page 98, using white paper or cotton.
7. Prepare the bowls from the patterns on pages 85 and 88. Color as desired.

Materials and Supplies

yellow background
orange and black border
orange letters
white paper
colored paper—brown, red, yellow,
  and orange

thin dinner-size paper plates
scissors
crayons
glue

Instructions

1. Discuss things for which the children are thankful. Have the children draw pictures of these things.
2. Place a black border around each child's picture.
3. Prepare the turkeys from the patterns on page 84. Use a paper plate for the body. Add feathers and feet made from brown, red, orange, and yellow paper. Glue the head, feathers, and feet to the body.

Materials and Supplies

light-blue background
brown grocery bags or any brown
    paper
tempera paints
sticks

manila paper
crayons
scissors
glue
Scotch Magic™ Tape

Instructions

1. Read about Indian tribes.
2. Prepare the tepee by gluing together brown paper or grocery bags to form a triangle larger than a small bulletin board. Paint Indian designs on the outside of the tepee, and paint the interior black. Also paint a black line along the open flap.
3. Tape the sticks in place.
4. Prepare the figures from the patterns on pages 75–78. The figures shown here are Western Blackfeet Indians. Color the figures heavily. Extend the figures and tepee beyond the borders of the bulletin board and tape, or tape the entire display to a wall.

Materials and Supplies

light-blue background
brown border and letters
dinner-size paper plate
white paper
colored paper—red, yellow, orange,
    and brown

crayons
scissors
glue
broad-tipped brown marker

Instructions

1. Read about and discuss turkeys.
2. Prepare the turkey from a pattern on page 84, using the paper plate and the red, orange, brown, and yellow paper. Cut and glue. Color the eye black.
3. Make labels from white paper, cutting three 3x9-inch strips and ten 3x12-inch strips. Use the marker to outline the labels and to print the following words on the 3x9-inch strips: tom, hen, poult. On the 3x12-inch strips print: body, head, neck, eye, mouth, wattle, wing, feathers, tail, and feet.

MAYFLOWER

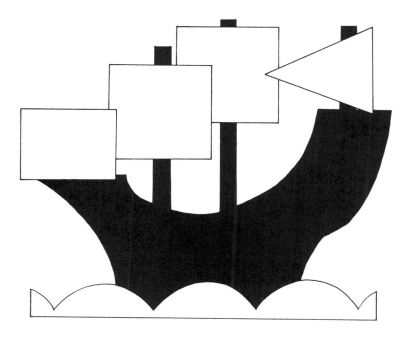

Materials and Supplies

black letters	glue
white paper	pencil
colored paper—black and blue	yardstick
tracing paper	ruler
newspapers	broad-tipped black marker
black and white tempera paints	Scotch Magic™ Tape
scissors	

Instructions

1. Read about the Pilgrims and Mayflower.
2. Prepare the ship from the pattern on page 83, using black paper for the ship and white paper for the sails.
3. Cut and glue the sails to the masts. Outline the sails with black marker.
4. Using a pencil and ruler, create a 7x9-inch grid of one-inch squares on the tracing paper. There will be 63 squares in all. Lay the grid on the small Mayflower.
5. Glue enough newspapers together to cover a 7x9-foot area. Create a grid by marking off the paper into one-foot squares. There will be 63 squares in all.
6. Using the small ship and grid as a guide, reproduce the Mayflower on the large grid. Duplicate the line(s) you see within each small square in the corresponding large square.
7. Paint the ship black and the sails white.
8. Cut out the ship and tape it to the wall.
9. Prepare the waves (quantity optional) from the pattern on page x, using blue paper. Glue in place.

Materials and Supplies

medium-blue background
black border and letters
white paper
colored paper—light-brown, green,
   yellow, and black construction
   paper

scissors
crayons
glue
broad-tipped black marker

Instructions

1. Read about and discuss the meaning of Christmas.
2. Prepare the tree trunks and walking staff from the patterns on page 87, using light-brown paper.
3. Prepare the manger and stable from the patterns on page 87, using black paper.
4. Prepare the leaves from the pattern on page 87, using green paper. Glue the leaves on the tree trunks.
5. Prepare the figures, angels, and baby Jesus from the patterns on pages 75, 76, and 87, respectively, using white paper. Color heavily and cut out. Glue the baby in the manger.
6. Prepare the star from the pattern on page 87, using yellow paper.
7. Prepare the sheep from the pattern on page 87, using white and black paper.
8. Outline all the shapes in black marker.

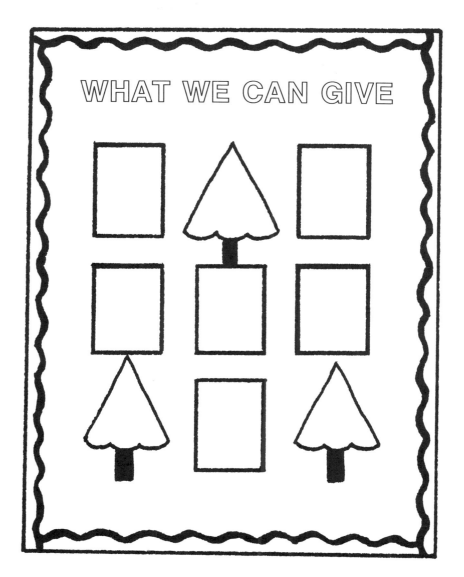

Materials and Supplies

red background
white border and letters
white paper (lined or unlined)
colored paper—black and green
crayons

scissors
glue
glitter (optional)
yellow or gold paper for menorahs
    (alternate option)

Instructions

1. Discuss ways people can give of themselves rather than buying gifts for loved ones. Allow the children to write about their ideas or to draw pictures.
2. Prepare the tree trunks from the pattern on page 86, using black paper.
3. Prepare the crowns from the pattern on page 86, using green paper. Glue the crowns on the tree trunks. Add ornaments from the pattern on page 96.
4. As an alternate option, prepare the menorahs from the pattern on page 88, using yellow or gold paper.

Materials and Supplies

dark-blue background
gold wrapping (or yellow) paper for
  border and letters
manila or white paper
colored paper—gold or yellow
light-brown paper, wood-grain
  contact paper, or grocery bag

white cloth
wrapping paper
ribbon
crayons
glue
scissors
Scotch Magic™ Tape

Instructions

1. Discuss Hanukkah. Have the children write or draw pictures about the holiday.
2. Prepare the table from the pattern on page 84, using light-brown paper, wood-grain contact paper, or a grocery bag.
3. Prepare the tablecloth from the pattern on page 88, using white (or any color) paper or cloth.
4. Prepare the menorah from the pattern on page 88, using gold or yellow paper.
5. Prepare the dishes from the patterns on pages 85 and 88, using manila or white paper. Color heavily.
6. Prepare the figures from the patterns on pages 75–78, using manila or white paper. Color heavily.
7. Prepare the packages by cutting wrapping paper and ribbon. Box sizes are optional. Glue or tape the ribbons to the wrapping paper.
8. Prepare the dreidel from the pattern on page 88, using manila or white paper. Color heavily.

Materials and Supplies

yellow background
green border and letters
colored paper—green and light-
   brown
wrapping paper

ribbon
crayons
scissors
Scotch Magic™ Tape

Instructions

1. Discuss comparison words: big, bigger, biggest.
2. Prepare the pine trees from the pattern on page 92, using green paper. Make three trees altogether, each one a little larger than the previous one. Color the trunks black.
3. Prepare the cookies from the pattern on page 89, using light-brown paper. Make three cookies altogether, each one a little larger than the previous one. Color decorations heavily with crayons.
4. Prepare the packages by cutting rectangles from wrapping paper. Start with a 6x8-inch rectangle, and then cut two more, each a little larger than the previous one. Decorate the packages as desired by taping on ribbons.

December

Materials and Supplies

dark-green background
white border and letters
white paper
colored paper—light-brown, light-
   green, yellow, and red
wrapping paper

ribbon
gold or silver paper (optional)
scissors
crayons
Scotch Magic™ Tape

Instructions

1. Read and talk about holidays and their symbols.
2. Prepare the cookie from the pattern on page 89, using light-brown paper. Color heavily.
3. Prepare the dreidel and candy cane from the patterns on page 88, using white paper. Color heavily.
4. Prepare the angel and Santa from the pattern on page 76, using white paper. Color heavily.
5. Prepare the star from the pattern on page 87, using yellow paper.
6. Prepare the sheep from the pattern on page 87, using white paper and black paper.
7. Prepare the packages by cutting shapes from wrapping paper (sizes optional) and taping on ribbons.
8. Prepare the bell from the pattern on page 88, using red paper.
9. Prepare the tree from the pattern on page 86, using light-green paper for the crown and black for the trunk.
10. Prepare the manger from the pattern on page 87, using light-brown paper.
11. Prepare the baby Jesus and the pancakes from the patterns on pages 87 and 88, respectively, using white paper. Color with crayons.
12. Prepare the menorah from the pattern on page 88, using yellow, gold, or silver paper.

December

Materials and Supplies

dark-green background
white and red borders
  (offset with red
  behind white)
white letters
manila and white paper
colored paper—yellow,
  light-blue,
  red, and light-brown
crayons
scissors
broad-tipped black marker
grocery bag (optional)

Instructions

1. Discuss the five senses.
2. Prepare the face from the pattern on page 88, using manila or light-brown paper or the grocery bag. Color heavily.
3. Prepare the star from the pattern on page 87, using yellow paper.
4. Prepare the cookie from the pattern on page 89, using light-brown paper or the grocery bag. Decorate as desired. Color heavily.
5. Prepare the candy cane from the pattern on page 88, using white paper. Color heavy red stripes.
6. Prepare the hand from the pattern on page 89, using manila or light-brown paper or the grocery bag. Color heavily.
7. Prepare the water drops from the pattern on page 88, using light-blue paper.
8. Prepare the bell from the pattern on page 88, using red paper.
9. Outline all the shapes in marker.
10. Add white paper strips to connect eyes, ears, nose, hand, and tongue to star, bell, cookie, raindrops, and candy cane, respectively.

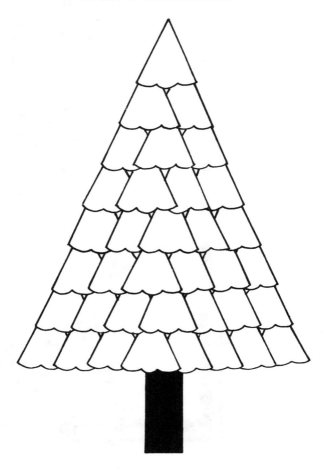

Materials and Supplies

white paper
colored paper (any kind—
    construction, wrapping, or
    painted newspaper)—green and
    black
colored magazines (optional)

scissors
glue
crayons
tempera paints (optional)
Scotch Magic™ Tape

Instructions

1. Read and talk about Christmas.
2. Prepare the crown by cutting 36 triangles or more from the pattern on page 86, using green paper. Glue together at the glue lines, keeping points straight up.
3. Prepare the tree trunk by cutting a 4x11-inch rectangle, using black paper. Glue behind and at the bottom of the assembled crowns.
4. Prepare the ornaments from the pattern on page 86, using wrapping paper, colored magazine ads, construction paper, or white paper colored heavily.
5. Prepare a star from the pattern on page 87, using yellow paper.
6. Tape the display to the wall.

January

WE HAVE FUN IN WINTER

Materials and Supplies

light-blue background
black border (points turned out
    toward wall) and letters
white and manila paper
colored paper—black and dark-blue
newspapers (optional)

crayons
scissors
broad-tipped black marker
glue
black and blue tempera paints
    (optional)

Instructions

1. Discuss winter.
2. Prepare the trees from the patterns on pages 74 and 81, using black paper or newspaper painted black.
3. Prepare the ice by cutting an oblong shape (size optional) from dark-blue paper or newspaper painted blue.
4. Prepare the figures from the patterns on pages 75–78, using manila paper. Color heavily.
5. Prepare the sled from the pattern on page 90. Color heavily.
6. Prepare the snowman and snowball from the patterns on pages 86 and 103, using white paper. Glue the parts of the snowman together.
7. Prepare the tree snow, using white paper. Cut to fit.
8. Outline all shapes in black.

Materials and Supplies

light-blue background
white border (edged with broad-
tipped black marker and inside
white border reversed, with flat
edge showing)
black letters

black paper or wide black bias tape
pictures of well-known black people
stories about George Washington
Carver, Martin Luther King, Jr.,
or other famous black people

Instructions

1. Place the black paper and bias tape (or strips of black paper) on the bulletin board.
2. Glue the pictures of black personalities on white paper. Offset the white paper on black paper.
3. Discuss the black people shown in the pictures.
4. Have the children write about or draw pictures of their favorite black people.

Materials and Supplies

light-blue background
white and dark-blue borders (dark-
   blue border placed so that it
   shows beyond white border)
dark-blue letters
white paper
brown paper (optional)

scissors
crayons
glue
broad-tipped black and dark-blue
   markers
magazine ads
dark-blue bias tape or paper

Instructions

1. Discuss the body's needs for a proper diet, emphasizing the four food groups.
2. Prepare the figure from the pattern on page 76, using white or brown paper. Color heavily. Outline in black.
3. Make the word labels by cutting four 4x16-inch strips of white paper. Use the dark-blue marker to print the following words on the labels: meats, nuts; milk, cheese; fruits, vegetables; and cereals, bread. Outline each label.
4. Add connecting lines made from strips of dark-blue paper or bias tape.
5. Cut colored magazine pictures of foods representing the four groups, and glue the pictures on 12 sheets of 9x12-inch white paper.

Materials and Supplies

dark-blue background
dark-blue and white border
 (white border turned toward
 blue border)
white letters
manila or white paper
colored paper—yellow, orange,
 red, and light-blue (or
 colored magazine ads)
scissors
crayons
glue
broad-tipped dark-blue marker

Instructions

1. Discuss clothing appropriate to each season.
2. Prepare the figures from the pattern on page 76, using manila or white paper. Color heavily.
3. Prepare the little leaves from the pattern on page 82, using orange, red, and yellow paper or colorful magazine ads.
4. Prepare the little snowflakes from the pattern on page 90, using white paper.
5. Prepare the raindrops from the pattern on page 88, using light-blue paper.
6. Prepare the sun from the pattern on page 102, using yellow paper. Glue behind the summer figure.
7. Prepare the waves from the pattern on page x, using light-blue paper. Glue at the feet of the summer figure.
8. Make four 3x10-inch labels from white paper. Use the dark-blue marker to print the following words: autumn, winter, spring, summer.

January

Materials and Supplies

light-blue background
green border (reversed) and letters
colored paper—black, yellow, dark-
   blue, pink, white, orange, brown,
   red, and several shades of green

broad-tipped green marker
scissors
glue

Instructions

1. Read and talk about the seasons.
2. Prepare the tree trunks from the pattern on page 74, using black paper.
3. Prepare the tree crowns from the pattern on page 74, using yellow, orange, red, brown paper (autumn), light-green shades of paper (spring), and dark-green shades of paper (summer).
4. Prepare small autumn leaves from the pattern on page 82, using yellow, orange, red, and brown paper.
5. Prepare the cloud from the pattern on page 98, using dark-blue paper.
6. Prepare the flowers from the pattern on page 100, using pink paper. Glue to the spring tree crowns.
7. Prepare the sun from the pattern on page 102, using yellow paper.
8. Prepare the snowflakes from the pattern on page 90, using white paper.
9. Prepare the rain from the pattern on page 88, using dark-blue paper.
10. Make four 4x14-inch labels from white paper. Use the green marker to edge each label and to print the following words: AUTUMN, WINTER, SPRING, and SUMMER.

Materials and Supplies

yellow background
black and orange border
black letters
cotton balls
small paper sack
white or manila paper
colored paper—yellow,
   red, orange,
   brown, and dark-blue
scissors
glue
crayons
string

Instructions

1. Read about and discuss ears and hearing.
2. Prepare the bus from the pattern on page 96. Color heavily.
3. Prepare the star from the pattern on page 87, using yellow paper.
4. Prepare the cat from the pattern on page 93. Color heavily.
5. Prepare the big leaves from the pattern on page 82, using red, orange, and yellow paper.
6. Prepare the face from the pattern on page 106, using white or brown paper. Color heavily.
7. Prepare the bell from the pattern on page 88, using red paper.
8. Prepare the bird from the pattern on page 90. Color heavily.
9. Prepare the dog from the pattern on page 93. Color heavily.
10. Prepare the raindrops from the pattern on page 88, using dark-blue paper.
11. Prepare the hen from the pattern on page 96. Color heavily.
12. Make the owl from a small paper sack. Add yellow eyes, beaks, and feet, black eyes, and brown feathers. Color heavily. Tie the feet with string.
13. Glue each picture to a black paper background cut slightly larger than the picture.

January

WHAT IS WINTER?

Materials and Supplies

black letters
black paper or newspapers
white paper
colored paper—green, red, and brown
blue paper (optional)
cotton (optional)

crayons
scissors
glue
black and blue tempera paints (optional)
wood-grain contact paper (optional)
broad-tipped black marker
Scotch Magic™ Tape

Instructions

1. Read about and discuss winter, animals, and animal tracks.
2. Prepare the tree trunks and branches from the patterns on pages 91 and 92, respectively, using black paper (or newspapers painted black) or wood-grain contact paper. Glue in place.
3. Prepare the pine trees from the pattern on page 92, using green and black paper.
4. Prepare the ground surface by cutting an oval from light-blue paper or newspapers painted light blue. Size is optional.
5. Prepare the rabbit from the pattern on page 90, using brown paper. Color heavily.
6. Prepare the rabbit tracks from the pattern on page 103, using black paper.
7. Prepare the birds from the pattern on page 90, using red paper. Add a large eye cut from black paper and feet cut from yellow paper.
8. Prepare the bird tracks from the pattern on page 90, using black paper.
9. Prepare the big snowflakes from the pattern on page 90, using white paper.
10. Prepare the snow, using cotton or white paper. Cut to fit trees.
11. Outline the shapes in marker.
12. Tape the entire display to the wall.

February

Materials and Supplies

yellow background   scissors
red border and letters   crayons
white paper   glue
colored paper—red

Instructions

1. Talk about love and the people, pets, and other things we love. Ask the children, "How do we show love?"
2. Prepare the big hearts from the pattern on page 94, using red paper. The number of hearts is optional.
3. Give the children white paper and have them color pictures of people, pets, and other things they love. Tell the children to color heavily and then to cut out and glue their pictures on the hearts.

Materials and Supplies

yellow background
red border and letters
white paper
colored paper—black and red

scissors
glue
broad-tipped black marker
3x5-inch cards (quantity optional)

Instructions

1. Prepare the trees from the pattern on page 74, using black paper.
2. Prepare the little hearts from the pattern on page 94, using red paper. The number of hearts is optional. Glue the hearts on the heart trees.
3. Make the card pockets from six 2½ x 5-inch cards. Outline each card pocket in black marker.
4. Make four 2½ x 4-inch number cards for each pocket. On one of the cards for each pocket, write the correct number of hearts on the tree. On the other three cards for each pocket, write incorrect numbers.

February

Materials and Supplies

light-blue background

dark-blue border and letters

white paper

colored paper—yellow, green, red, orange, gray, and brown

glue

scissors

crayons

broad-tipped black marker

Instructions

1. Discuss shadows, especially in regard to Groundhog Day (February 2).
2. Prepare the figure from the pattern on page 76, using white or brown paper. Color heavily.
3. Prepare the trees from the patterns on pages 74 and 87. Use brown paper for the trunks and green paper for the crowns. Glue the crowns to the trunks.
4. Prepare the bell from the pattern on page 88, using red paper.
5. Prepare the candy cane from the pattern on page 88, using white paper. Color in heavy red stripes.
6. Prepare the cat from the pattern on page 93, using brown, black, gray, or orange paper.
7. Prepare the big heart from the pattern on page 94, using red paper.
8. Prepare the sun from the pattern on page 102, using yellow paper.
9. Make the shadows by drawing around each object on gray paper and cutting out the shapes.
10. Outline all the shapes in black marker.

Materials and Supplies

light-blue background
dark-blue and red border
dark-blue letters
white paper
colored paper—red,
   yellow, green,
   black, brown,
   and orange
scissors
broad-tipped black marker

Instructions

1. Talk about things that need sun and water.
2. Prepare the fish from the pattern on page 94, using orange paper.
3. Prepare the big heart from the pattern on page 94, using red paper.
4. Prepare the hamster from the pattern on page 94, using brown paper.
5. Prepare the cat from the pattern on page 93, using black and white paper. Color heavily.
6. Prepare the dog from the pattern on page 93, using black and white paper.
7. Prepare the trash can from the pattern on page 78, using brown paper.
8. Prepare the ghost and star from the patterns on pages 82 and 87, respectively, using white paper.
9. Prepare the tree from the pattern on page 74, using black and green paper.
10. Prepare the boy from the pattern on page 76, using white or brown paper. Color heavily.
11. Prepare the bird from the pattern on page 97, using white paper.
12. Prepare the bell from the pattern on page 88, using red paper.
13. Prepare the sheep from the pattern on page 100, using white paper. Color the sheep's face and feet black.
14. Outline all the shapes in black marker.

Materials and Supplies

yellow background
red border and letters
manila or white paper
crayons
glue
broad-tipped red marker

writing paper (optional)
pet feed
plastic sandwich bags
string
Scotch Magic™ Tape

Instructions

1. Read about and discuss care of pets.
2. Prepare the following pets, using manila or white paper. Color heavily with any colors desired.
   turkey (from pattern on page 84)
   small sheep (from pattern on page 87)
   rabbit (from pattern on page 90)
   bird (from pattern on page 97)
   dog and cat (from patterns on page 93)
   hamster, turtle, fish (from patterns on page 94)
   hen (from pattern on page 96)
   puppy (from pattern on page 98)
   big sheep, chicks, bunnies, kitten (from patterns on page 100)
   pig (from pattern on page 102)
   cow and snake (from patterns on page 103)
   duck (from pattern on page 106)
   fish (from pattern on page 94)
3. Make up small bags of pet feed, tie closed, and attach to the pictures with tape.
4. As an optional activity, ask the children to write about proper pet care. Glue their reports to the bottoms of the pictures.
5. Outline all the sheets of paper in red marker.

Materials and Supplies

pink background
red border along outside edge,
   white border reversed toward red
   border
red letters
white and red paper

pictures of Washington, Lincoln,
   and recent presidents (optional)
broad-tipped black marker
scissors
manila paper (optional)

Instructions

1. Read about and discuss the presidents.
2. Display pictures of the presidents in oblongs of white paper, outlined in black.
3. Place the four white oblongs on a larger oblong of red paper.

February

BE MY VALENTINE

Materials and Supplies

red letters
red and black paper or newspapers
red and black tempera paints
  (optional)

scissors
glue
Scotch Magic™ Tape

Instructions

1. Discuss Valentine's Day.
2. Prepare the trees from the patterns on pages 91 and 92, using black paper or newspapers painted black. Glue the branches to the trunks.
3. Prepare the big hearts from the pattern on page 94, using red paper or newspapers painted red. Glue to the trees.
4. Tape the display to the wall.

March

Materials and Supplies

light-blue background
dark-blue border and letters
manila and white paper
crayons

scissors
glue
broad-tipped dark-blue marker

Instructions

1. Read about birds.
2. Prepare the birds from the patterns on pages 90 and 97, using manila paper. Color heavily and cut out.
3. Make the labels by cutting eight $4\frac{1}{2}$ x 9-inch strips of white paper and printing the following words in dark-blue marker (or cutting and gluing dark-blue letters): head, body, bones, feathers, eyes, beak, wings, and tail. Outline the labels in dark-blue marker.

Materials and Supplies

light-blue background
dark-blue border
  and letters
manila or white paper
colored paper—brown,
  black, and yellow
crayons
glue
doll clothes
heavy cord
clothespins
pins
broad-tipped black marker

Instructions

1. Read the poem "Who Has Seen The Wind?" by Christina Rosetti. Ask the students to think about the wind and what it does.
2. Prepare the tree trunk and leaves from the patterns on pages 74 and 82, respectively, using black and brown paper.
3. Prepare the figures from the patterns on pages 75 and 76, using manila or white paper. Color heavily and cut out.
4. Prepare the house from the pattern on page 97, using yellow paper. Add black windows and doors, red chimney, and brown roof. Color heavily.
5. Prepare the kite from the pattern on page 95, using white paper. Color heavily and glue on string.
6. Prepare the smoke from the pattern on page 97, using black paper.
7. Pin a length of heavy cord in place for the clothesline.
8. Attach doll clothes to the cord with clothespins. Pin the clothes at an angle to make it appear as if they are blowing in the wind.

Materials and Supplies

green background
red border, reversed, and letters
small paper sacks
white paper
red paper

crayons
scissors
glue
newspaper (optional)
red tempera paint (optional)

Instructions

1. Read about and discuss what Red Cross workers do.
2. Make the workers from paper sacks. Color in the hair, eyes, and top of mouth on each sack bottom. Color in the bottom of the mouth and chin on the side of the sack. Below each chin, color in a blue dress or jumpsuit.
3. Prepare the protective helmets from the pattern on page 96, using white paper. Add red crosses; then glue to heads (sack bottoms).
4. Prepare the large cross, using red paper or newspapers painted red. The size of the cross is optional.
5. Cut small pieces of white paper for the name tags. Add red crosses; then glue on sacks.

March

Materials and Supplies

yellow background

dark-green border, reversed, and
    letters

white paper

colored paper—dark-green

scissors

crayons

glue

broad-tipped green marker

Instructions

1. Read about or discuss St. Patrick. Explain that he was a missionary to Ireland, winning over many people to Christianity. In the United States, St. Patrick's Day is celebrated on March 17 with parades and people wearing green to honor Ireland.
2. Prepare the figure from the pattern on page 76, using brown paper (the probable color of his coat). Color heavily.
3. Prepare the shamrocks from the pattern on page 95, using green paper. Cut four leaves, overlap them slightly, and glue to the stem. For a 3-D effect, bend the centers on the dotted lines.
4. Cut strips of white paper for the labels. Size is optional. Use green marker to outline the labels and to print the words MISSIONARY TO IRELAND.

Materials and Supplies

orchid or white background
purple border and letters
manila paper
colored paper—brown, yellow, and
  purple

crayons
scissors
writing paper (optional)
white chalk
broad-tipped purple marker

Instructions

1. Discuss Easter customs. Have the children write or draw pictures about Easter. Outline their papers in purple marker.
2. Prepare the eggs from the pattern on page 99. Color heavily.
3. Prepare the rabbits from the pattern on page 90, using brown paper. Use chalk to make the white of the eye and a black crayon to make the center and outer edge.
4. Prepare the chicks from the pattern on page 100, using yellow paper. Add orange feet and beaks and black eyes.
5. Offset purple paper behind the children's writing or drawings.

Materials and Supplies

light-blue background
black border and letters
white paper
colored paper—brown,
    red, black,
    yellow, and green
crayons
scissors
glue
broad-tipped
    black marker

Instructions

1. Read about and discuss animal babies.
2. Prepare the hen from the pattern on page 96, using white paper. Add a red comb and face and a black eye. Place the hen on a yellow nest.
3. Prepare the sheep from the patterns on pages 87 and 100, using white paper. Color in heavily black legs and face.
4. Prepare the bears from the pattern on page 98, using brown paper. Add black eyes.
5. Prepare the bird from the pattern on page 90, using red paper. Add a yellow beak and legs and a black eye.
6. Prepare the tree from the pattern on page 74, using black paper.
7. Prepare the bird nest from the pattern on page 99, using brown paper. Make the birds red. Glue the nest in the tree.
8. Prepare the turtles from the pattern on page 94, using brown and black paper.
9. Prepare the chicks from the pattern on page 100, using yellow paper. Add orange legs and beak and a black eye.
10. Prepare the cat from the pattern on page 93. Color heavily.
11. Prepare the kittens from the pattern on page 100. Color heavily.
12. Prepare the dog and puppy from the patterns on pages 93 and 98, respectively. Color heavily.
13. Outline all the shapes in black marker.

April

Materials and Supplies

light-blue background
dark-green border and letters
white paper
colored paper—various shades of
   light-green, pink, yellow, black,
   brown, and dark-blue
scissors

colored magazines (optional)
wallpaper (optional)
pink and yellow tissue paper
   (optional)
glue
broad-tipped green marker

Instructions

1. Discuss spring.
2. Prepare the tree trunks from the pattern on page 74, using black or brown paper or wallpaper.
3. Prepare the crowns from the pattern on page 74, using shades of light-green paper or wallpaper.
4. Prepare the little flowers from the pattern on page 100, using pink and white paper or colored magazine ads, wallpaper, or crumpled tissue paper. Glue the flowers to each other and to the trees.
5. Prepare the raindrops and the clouds from the patterns on pages 88 and 98, respectively, using dark-blue paper.
6. Prepare the bird and nest from the patterns on pages 90 and 99, respectively, using white paper. Color heavily.

April

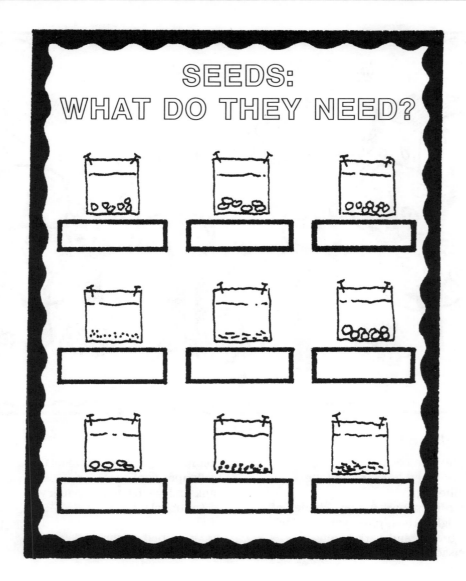

Materials and Supplies

light-green background
dark-green border and letters
white paper
sandwich bags

broad-tipped dark-green marker
seeds
pins

Instructions

1. Read about seeds and discuss how they are used and what is needed to make them grow.
2. Make up a separate bag for each seed variety. Pin the bags to the bulletin board.
3. Cut nine 3x9-inch strips of white paper for labels. Print the names of the seed varieties on the labels. Outline each label in dark-green marker.

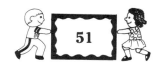

Materials and Supplies

medium-blue background
dark-green border and letters
white paper
colored paper—brown, green, and
   dark-green

newspapers (optional)
brown tempera paint (optional)
crayons
glue
writing or drawing paper

Instructions

1. Discuss the meaning of Easter. Have the children write or draw pictures about the holiday.
2. Make the cross from brown paper or newspaper painted brown. Draw in wood-grain lines. Make the horizontal bar 7x24 inches, the vertical bar 7x31 inches. Glue the bars together.
3. Prepare the flowers from the pattern on page 100, using green and white paper. Color in orange stamens.
4. Offset dark-green paper behind the children's writing or drawings.

April

Materials and Supplies

medium-blue background
dark-blue border and letters
white and manila paper
colored paper—light-brown and
    dark-blue
scissors

crayons
glue
broad-tipped black marker
wallpaper and writing paper
    (optional)

Instructions

1. Discuss Passover. Have the children write or draw pictures about the holiday.
2. Prepare the figures from the patterns on pages 75–77, using manila paper. Color heavily.
3. Prepare the table from the pattern on page 84, using light-brown paper or wallpaper.
4. Prepare the tablecloth from the pattern on page 88, using white paper. Color as desired.
5. Prepare the matzos from the pattern on page 99. Color as desired.
6. Prepare the book from the pattern on page 99. Color heavily.
7. Outline all the shapes in black marker.
8. Offset sheets of dark-blue paper behind the children's writing or drawings.

Materials and Supplies

dark-blue letters
white paper
colored paper—black or brown,
    pink, yellow, blue, dark- blue,
    and various shades of green
newspapers or grocery bags
    (optional)

black, brown, green, blue tempera
    paints (optional)
colored magazine ads (optional)
crayons
scissors
glue
Scotch Magic™ Tape

Instructions

1. Discuss spring.
2. Prepare the tree trunks from the pattern on page 80, using black or brown paper (or newspapers or grocery bags painted brown or black). Cut out the shapes.
3. Prepare the crowns from the pattern on page 80, using shades of green paper (or newspapers or grocery bags painted green).
4. Prepare the big flowers from the pattern on page 98, using pink, white, and yellow paper or colored magazine ads.
5. Prepare the raindrops from the pattern on page 88, using dark-blue paper.
6. Make the puddles from blue paper or newspaper painted blue. The size of the puddles is optional.
7. Prepare the birds from the pattern on page 90, using white paper. Color as desired.
8. Prepare the nests from the pattern on page 99, using white paper or a grocery bag. Color heavily.
9. Prepare the big clouds from the pattern on page 112, using dark-blue paper.
10. Tape the display to the wall.

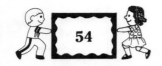

May

Materials and Supplies

light-blue background
black and green border
black letters
paper plate
white and manila paper
colored paper—red, yellow, gray,
   black, green, brown, orange, pink

wide green rickrack
cotton (optional)
scissors
crayons
glue
broad-tipped black marker

Instructions

1. Read about and discuss farms.
2. Prepare the house from the pattern on page 97, using yellow paper for the main structure. Add a gray roof and windows and a red door and chimney. Color heavily.
3. Prepare the trees from the pattern on page 74, using black and green paper. Glue the parts of the tree.
4. Prepare the pig from the pattern on page 102, using pink paper. Add black eyes and nostrils.
5. Prepare the sheep from the pattern on page 87, using white paper. Add black faces and legs.
6. Prepare the figures from the pattern on page 76, using white or brown paper. Color heavily.
7. Prepare the barn from the pattern on page 101, using red paper. Add a black door and gray roof.
8. Prepare the corn from the pattern on page 103, using green paper.
9. Prepare the cow from the pattern on page 103. Color as desired.
10. Prepare the clouds from the pattern on page 98, using white paper or cotton.
11. Prepare the birds from the pattern on page 90. Color as desired.
12. Make the grass from green rickrack.
13. Prepare the small turkey from the pattern on page 84, using a paper plate and brown, red, yellow, and orange paper.
14. Prepare the ducks from the pattern on page 106, using white paper. Add orange feet and bill and a black eye.
15. Prepare the chicks and the sun from the patterns on pages 100 and 102, respectively, using yellow paper. Add black eyes to the chicks.
16. Outline all the shapes in black marker.

Materials and Supplies

dark-green background
white border and letters
white paper
colored paper—light-blue

scissors
crayons
broad-tipped green marker

Instructions

1. Discuss short vowels.
2. Prepare the raindrops from the pattern on page 88, using light-blue paper.
3. Prepare the duck from the pattern on page 106, using white paper. Add orange feet and beak and a black eye.
4. Prepare the fish from the pattern on page 94. Color it orange.
5. Prepare the hen from the pattern on page 96, using white paper. Add a red face and comb and a yellow beak. Place the hen on a yellow nest.
6. Prepare the cat from the pattern on page 93. Color as desired.
7. Make five 3x6-inch labels from white paper. Use green marker to print the words: cat, hen, fish, drops, and duck.

Materials and Supplies

medium-blue background
black border and letters
white paper
colored paper—black, red, yellow,
  green, orange, brown, blue, and
  dark-blue

crayons
scissors
glue
broad-tipped black marker
thin dinner-size paper plate

Instructions

1. Talk about the months of the year.
2. Prepare the trees from the patterns on pages 74 and 86, using green and black paper.
3. Prepare the flower from the pattern on page 100, using white and green paper. Color the stamens orange.
4. Prepare the star and sun from the patterns on pages 87 and 102, respectively, using yellow paper. Glue the star to the top of the tree.
5. Prepare the big heart from the pattern on page 94, using red paper.
6. Prepare the little ghost from the pattern on page 81, using white paper. Add a black mouth and eyes.
7. Prepare the figures from the patterns on pages 75 and 76, using white or brown paper. Color heavily.
8. Prepare the little turkey from the pattern on page 84, using a paper plate and brown, red, yellow, and orange paper.
9. Prepare the raindrops and cloud from the patterns on pages 88 and 98, respectively, using dark-blue paper.
10. Prepare the little snowflakes from the pattern on page 90, using white paper.
11. Prepare the flag from the pattern on page 89. Color heavily.
12. Prepare the waves from the pattern on page x, using blue paper.
13. Prepare the book from the pattern on page 99. Color as desired. Glue in the child's hand.
14. Make labels from white paper. Label size is optional. Print the names of the months in black marker.
15. Outline all the shapes in black marker.

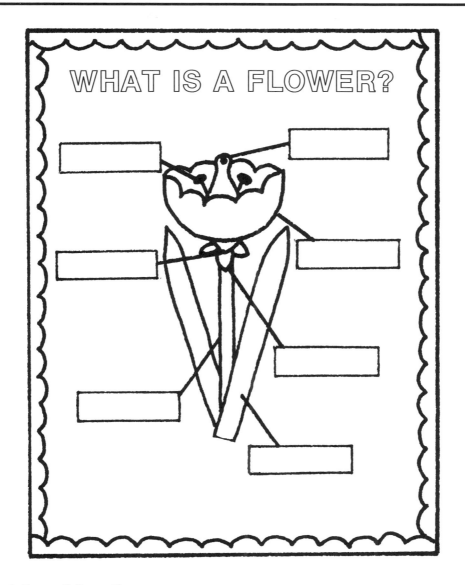

Materials and Supplies

dark-blue background
light-blue border and letters
white paper
colored paper—yellow and two
   shades of light-green

crayons
scissors
glue
broad-tipped dark-blue marker

Instructions

1. Read about flowers.
2. Prepare the flower from the pattern on page 102, using yellow paper for the petals. Color the stamens and pistil orange. Use two shades of green for the stem and for the leaves. Glue the parts of the flower.
3. Make seven 3x8-inch labels from white paper. Use a dark- blue marker to print the words: stamen, pistil, receptacle, petal, stem, sepals, and leaf.
4. Add strips of white paper as lines between the flower parts and the labels.

June

Materials and Supplies

orange background
dark-green border and letters
manila or white paper
colored paper—dark-green

crayons
scissors
writing paper (optional)

Instructions

1. Have the children write about or draw pictures about happy times and sad times.
2. Prepare the faces from the pattern on page 106, using manila, white, or brown paper. Color heavily.
3. Offset sheets of dark-green paper behind the children's writing or drawings.

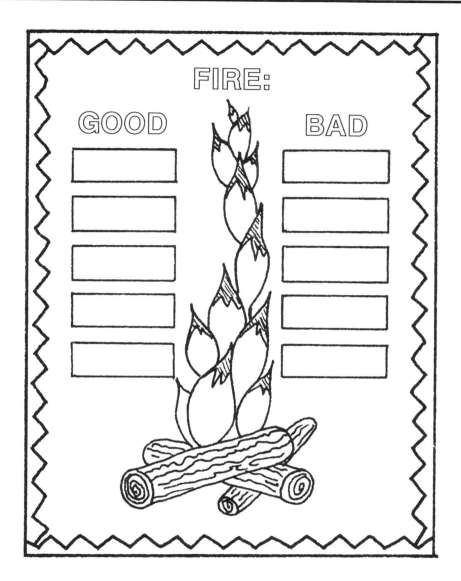

Materials and Supplies

dark-green background
orange border and letters
white paper
colored paper—light-brown

crayons
scissors
glue
broad-tipped orange marker

Instructions

1. Discuss fire and the ways fire is good and bad.
2. Prepare the logs from the pattern on page 105, using brown paper. Color heavy brown graining.
3. Prepare the flames from the pattern on page 105, using yellow paper. Add an orange tip to each flame. Glue the flames together.
4. Make 4x12-inch labels from white paper. Use orange marker to outline the labels and to print good and bad aspects of fire on them.

June

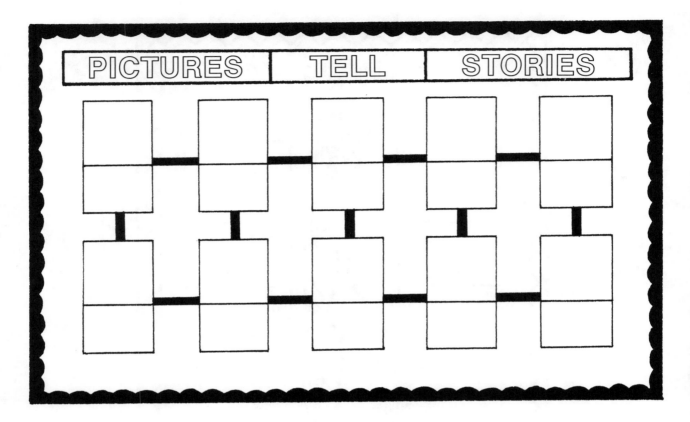

Materials and Supplies

light-blue background
dark-blue border and letters
pictures from magazines or
    newspapers (ones that will
    inspire writing)

white paper
writing paper
pencils
broad-tipped dark-blue marker

Instructions

1. Glue the pictures on white paper, and then display the pictures. Give the children time to think about the pictures and to make up stories about what they see. Then have them write their stories.
2. Attach the children's stories to the bottoms of the pictures. Outline the pictures and stories in blue marker. Display.

Materials and Supplies

dark-green background
orange border and letters
pictures of famous people
white paper

wide orange bias tape (optional)
broad-tipped orange marker
scissors
glue

Instructions

1. Cut pictures from newspapers and magazines. Glue the pictures in rectangles and circles of white paper. Connect the pictures with orange bias tape or strips of orange paper.
2. Outline each circle and square with the orange marker.
3. Discuss the identities of the people in the pictures. Ask the children what types of people are shown. Ask why the people are famous.

Materials and Supplies

light-blue background
dark-green border and letters
white or manila paper
colored paper—yellow, black, green,
  brown, and dark-blue

crayons
scissors
glue
broad-tipped black marker

Instructions

1. Read about and discuss summer.
2. Prepare the figures from the patterns on pages 75-78, 104, and 110, using white or brown paper. Color heavily.
3. Prepare the trees from the patterns on page 74, using green and black paper. Glue the tree parts.
4. Prepare the waves from the pattern on page x, using dark-blue and white paper. Glue.
5. Prepare the skateboard from the pattern on page 104. Color heavily. Glue to the figures.
6. Prepare the sun from the pattern on page 102, using yellow paper.
7. Prepare the basketball from the pattern on page 104, using brown paper.
8. Prepare the hoop from the pattern on page 104. Color as desired.
9. Prepare the book from the pattern on page 99. Color as desired. Glue the book to the figure.
10. Prepare the doll from the pattern on page 104. Color as desired. Glue the doll to the figure.
11. Outline all the shapes in black marker.

Materials and Supplies

yellow background

black border and letters

children's baby pictures

black paper

scissors

glue

pins

Instructions

1. Glue sheets of black paper together to form a large area. Then cut the black area into an irregular shape.
2. Secure the pictures to the black area with pins. Be careful to place the pins in the white area above and below each photo so as not to puncture the picture.
3. Let the children guess the identity of each baby.

Materials and Supplies

light-blue background
dark-blue border and letters
manila, brown, or white paper
crayons

scissors
glue
broad-tipped black marker

Instructions

1. Talk about Independence Day.
2. Prepare the figures from the patterns on pages 75–78, using brown, white, or manila paper. Color heavily.
3. Prepare the flags from the pattern on page 109. Color red, white, and blue.
4. Prepare the instruments from the pattern on page 109. Color heavily.
5. Prepare the fireworks from the pattern on page 107. Color heavily.
6. Outline all the shapes in black marker.

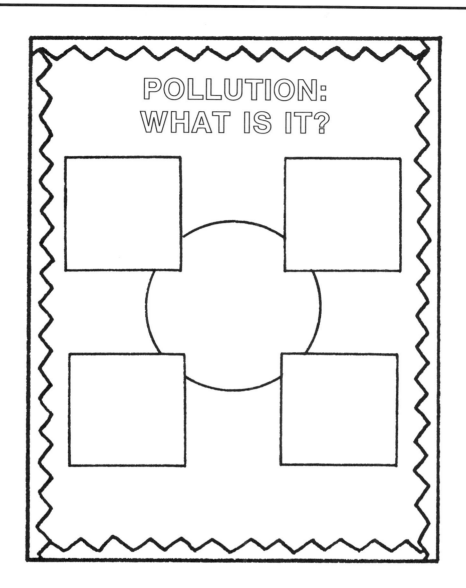

Materials and Supplies

orchid background
purple border and letters
white paper
colored paper—purple

scissors
glue
broad-tipped purple marker

Instructions

1. Cut pictures from newspapers or magazines that show pollution, or ask the children to bring in such pictures.
2. Glue the pictures within the circle and the squares.
3. Outline all the shapes in purple marker.
4. Discuss the causes and effects of pollution and what can be done about it. Talk about ways everyone can help.

July

OUR CLASS

Materials and Supplies

black background

yellow border and letters

manila, brown, and white paper

crayons

scissors

Instructions

1. Talk about how each class member is unique and how each has his or her good qualities. Emphasize the need for cooperation and good behavior in the classroom.
2. Prepare the faces from the patterns on page 106, using manila, brown, and white paper.
3. Have each child draw his or her face, coloring heavily.
4. Assemble the faces into a class montage.

July

Materials and Supplies

light-blue background
dark-blue border and letters
white paper
crayons

scissors
glue
broad-tipped blue marker

Instructions

1. Read about Uncle Sam (information can be found in encyclopedias), and discuss what he represents.
2. Prepare Uncle Sam from the patterns on pages 108 and 109, using white paper. Color heavily so that the white hat has a blue band with white stars, the tie and mouth are red, the coat and eyes are blue. Glue the hat in place.
3. Outline the shapes in dark-blue marker.
4. Make six 3x7-inch and one 3x14-inch labels from white paper. Use a dark-blue marker to outline each label and to print on the 3x7-inch labels: UNITED, STATES, NICKNAME, SYMBOL, 1812, and U. S. On the 3x14-inch label print: COLORS OF OUR FLAG.

August

Materials and Supplies

light-blue background
dark-blue border and letters
manila or white paper
yellow and various shades of blue
   paper
newspapers (optional)
grocery bags
blue and brown tempera paints
   (optional)

cotton (optional)
shells (optional)
crayons
scissors
glue
Scotch Magic™ Tape
broad-tipped black marker

Instructions

1. Read about and discuss the beach, ocean, and shells.
2. Prepare the figures from the patterns on pages 75–78, 104, and 110, using manila paper. Color heavily.
3. Prepare the surfboard, shells, pail and shovel from the patterns on pages 110 and 111. Color heavily.
4. Make the sand by gluing grocery bags together. Cut to whatever size and shape desired.
5. Prepare the waves from the pattern on page 112, using shades of blue paper or newspapers painted blue. Cut and glue the strips in place. The number of waves is optional.
6. Prepare the clouds from the pattern on page 98, using white paper or cotton.
7. Prepare the beach ball and umbrella from the patterns on pages 110 and 112, respectively. Color heavily.
8. Prepare the sun from the pattern on page 102, using yellow paper.
9. Tape real shells to the bulletin board (optional).
10. Prepare the book from the pattern on page 99. Color as desired.
11. Outline all the shapes in black marker.

WHAT IS A FISH?

Materials and Supplies

medium-blue background
dark-blue border and letters
white paper
crayons
scissors

white yarn
broad-tipped dark-blue marker
Scotch Magic™ Tape
clear plastic

Instructions

1. Read about and discuss fish.
2. Prepare the fish from the pattern on page 111, using white paper. Color the fish's body orange. Use a blue marker to outline the fish and make its eye, nostril, gill cover, fins, and scales.
3. Make eight 3x7-inch labels from white paper. Use a blue marker to outline each label and to print the words: nostril, eye, scales, mouth, fin, fins (2), and gill cover.
4. Connect labels and fish parts with white yarn.
5. Make three 4x14-inch labels from white paper. Use a blue marker to outline each label and to print these facts: Fish have backbones. They live in the water. Fish provide us with food.
6. To give the entire bulletin board an underwater effect, cover it with clear plastic.

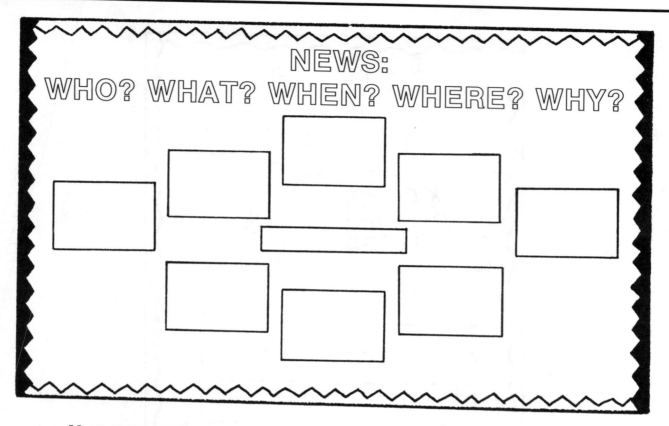

Materials and Supplies

dark-green background
orange and white border
white letters
nameplate of local newspaper

white paper
scissors
maps (optional)

Instructions

1. Display the nameplate from your local newspaper in the center of the bulletin board.
2. Cut newsworthy pictures from the newspaper, and ask the children to bring in newspaper pictures they find interesting. Tell the children to discuss the pictures at home before bringing them in so that they can talk knowledgeably about the pictures in class.
3. Glue the pictures on sheets of white paper.
4. Discuss WHO each picture is about, WHAT happened, WHEN it happened, WHERE it happened, and WHY it happened.
5. Encourage the children to use maps to find locations with which they are not familiar.

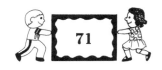
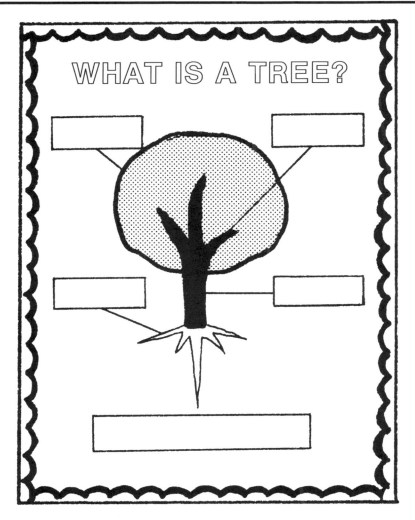

Materials and Supplies

yellow background
white and dark-green borders
   (white on the outside, green
   inside and showing beyond the
   white)
dark-green letters
brown, black, green, white paper

broad-tipped dark-green marker
scissors
glue
black bias tape (optional)

Instructions

1. Read about and discuss trees and how they are used.
2. Prepare the tree from the pattern on page 74, using black and green paper. Glue the tree parts together.
3. Prepare the roots from the pattern on page 89, using brown paper. Glue the roots to the tree.
4. Make four 3 x 9-inch labels from white paper. Use a dark-green marker to outline each label and to print the words crown, branch, roots, and trunk.
5. Make one 4 x 14-inch label. Use a dark-green marker to outline the label and to print the following fact: A TREE IS A PLANT.
6. Use bias tape or black paper strips to make lines between the labels and the tree parts.

August

Materials and Supplies

black letters
black and green paper (or
   newspapers or grocery bags)
white or manila paper
thin dinner-size paper plate
crayons

scissors
glue
blue and green tempera paints
   (optional)
cloth or wallpaper (optional)
broad-tipped black marker
Scotch Magic™ Tape

Instructions

1. Talk about vacations, picnics, lakes, and woods.
2. Prepare the figures from the patterns on pages 75–78, 104, and 110, using manila, white, or brown paper. Color heavily.
3. Prepare the trees from the patterns on pages 74, 81, and 86, using green and black paper. Glue the parts of the trees together.
4. Prepare the jug, ice chest, and sandwiches from the patterns on pages 102, 110, and 111, respectively. Color heavily.
5. Prepare the table and tablecloth from the patterns on pages 84 and 88, respectively. Color heavily.
6. Prepare the cloud from the pattern on page 112, using white paper.
7. Make the sun by coloring a dinner-size paper plate heavily in yellow.
8. Make the grass and water from green and blue paper (or from newspapers or grocery bags painted green and blue), respectively. The sizes of the grass and water are optional.
9. Outline all the shapes in black marker.
10. Tape the display to the wall.

PROJECT PATTERNS

Tree, Crown

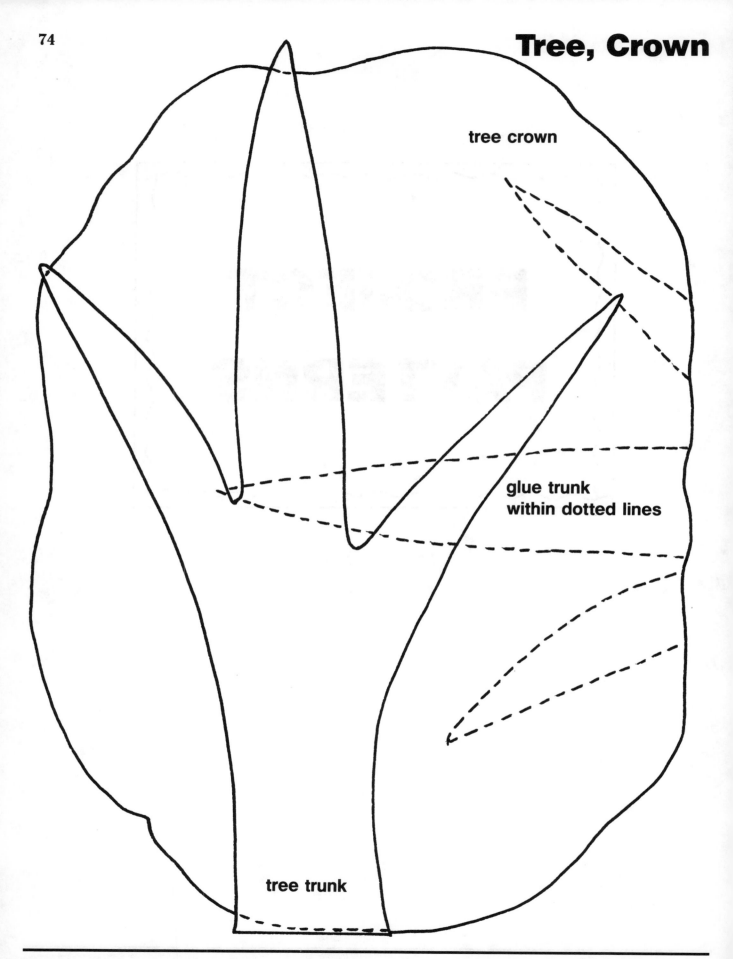

tree crown

glue trunk
within dotted lines

tree trunk

To reverse side
figure, trace,
cut, and
turn over.

Figure, Fruit

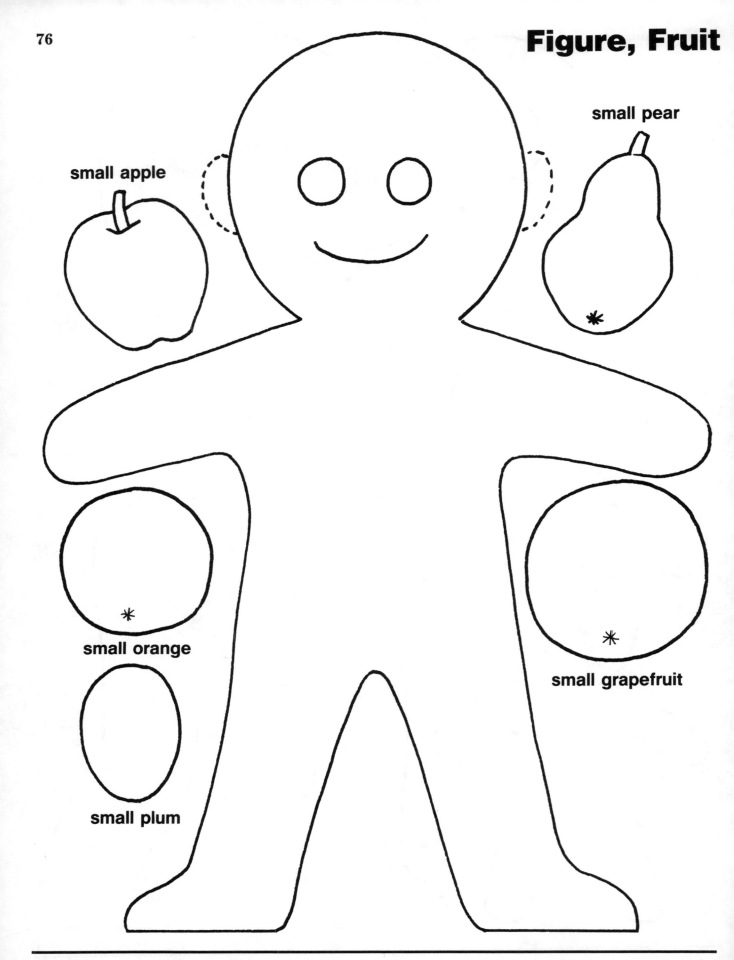

small apple

small pear

small orange

small grapefruit

small plum

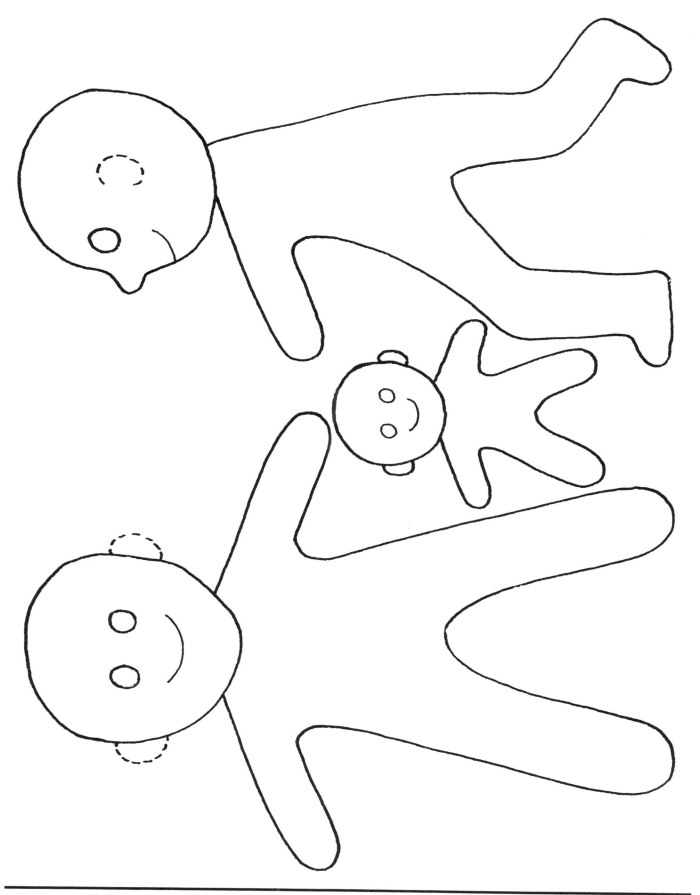

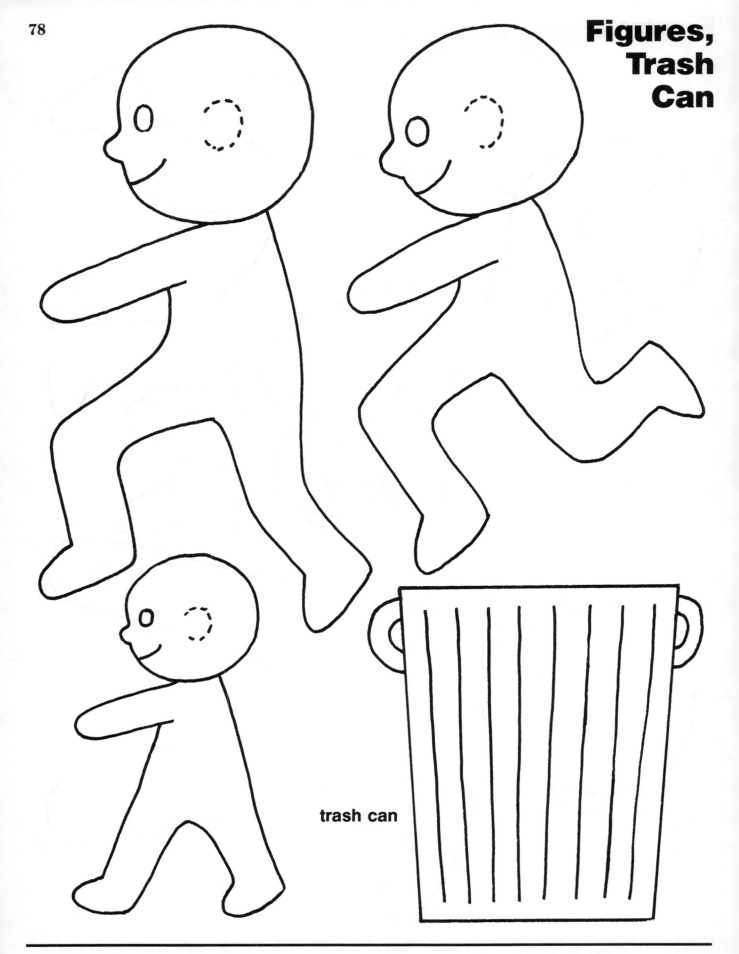

Figures, Trash Can

trash can

Traffic Light, Big Fruit

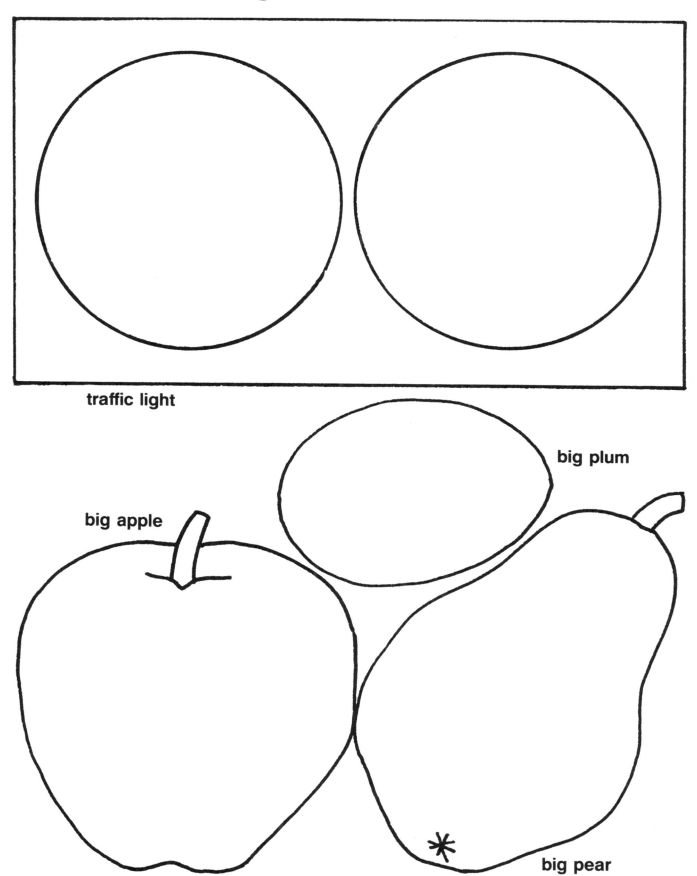

traffic light

big plum

big apple

big pear

Large Tree Trunk, Crown

tree trunk: Cut five 6½ x 9¾-inch shapes and glue together.

tree crown: Glue together sheets of green paper or use painted newspapers to make a 36-inch square. Shape and cut the crown. Glue to the trunk.

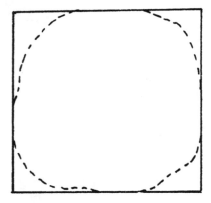

glue line

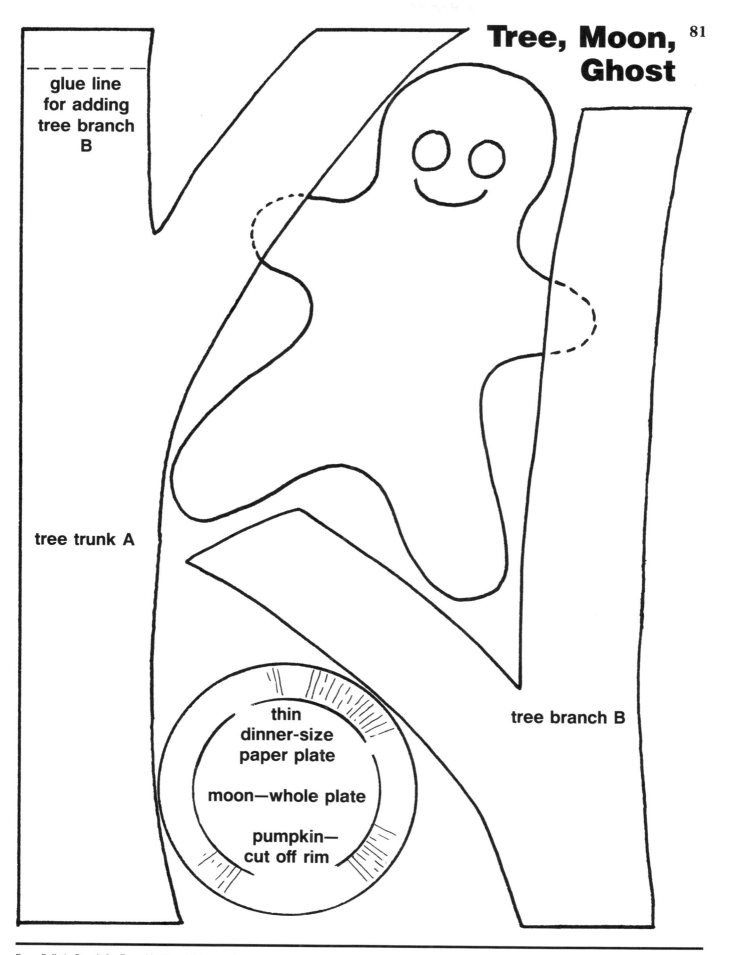

glue line
for adding
tree branch
B

tree trunk A

tree branch B

thin
dinner-size
paper plate

moon—whole plate

pumpkin—
cut off rim

Big Ghost, Leaves

little
leaf

big
leaf

big ghost

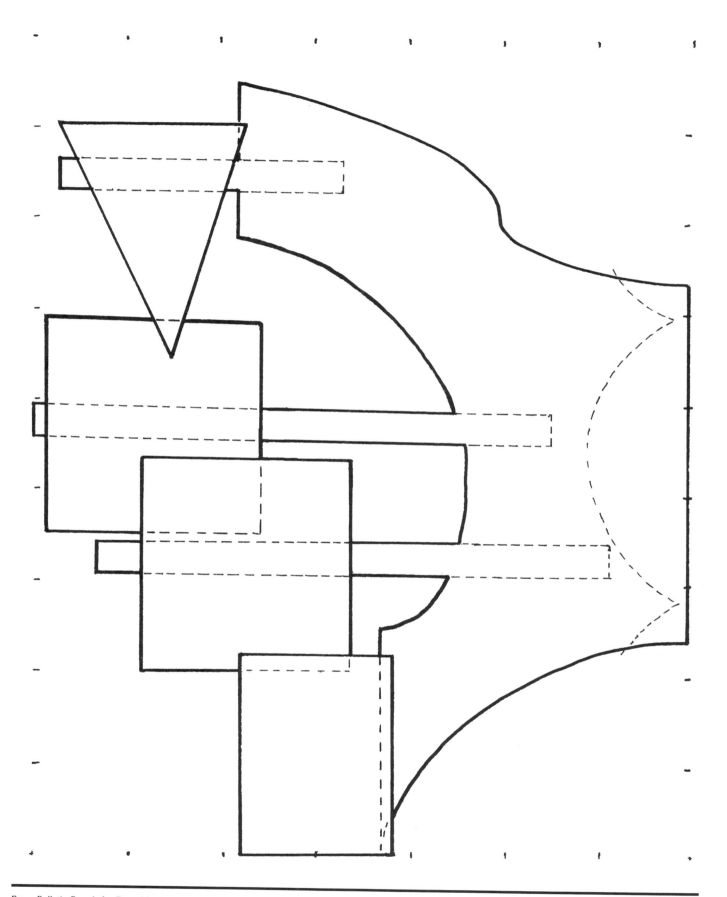

Turkeys, Table

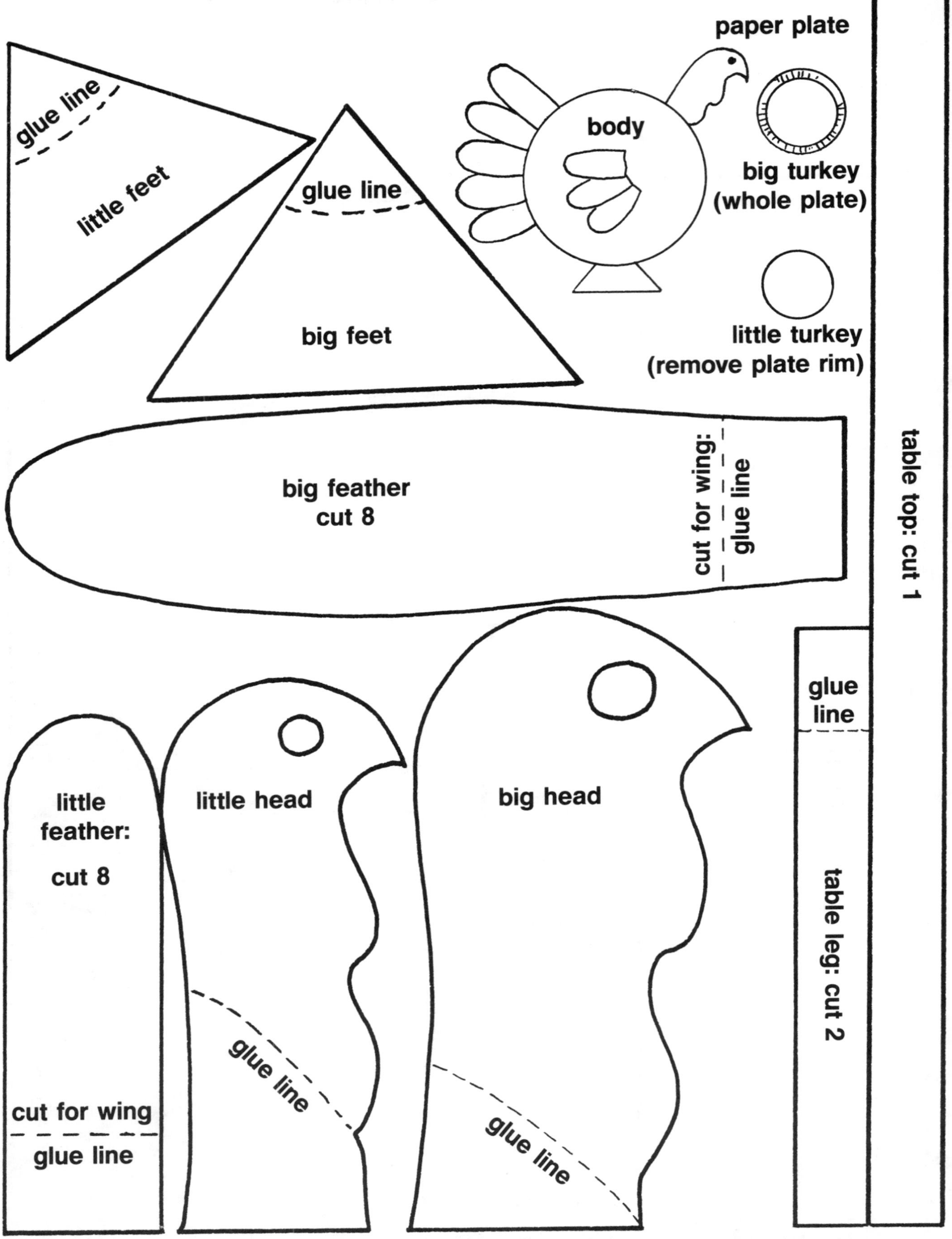

glue line

little feet

glue line

big feet

paper plate

body

big turkey
(whole plate)

little turkey
(remove plate rim)

big feather
cut 8

cut for wing:
glue line

table top: cut 1

little
feather:

cut 8

little head

big head

glue
line

table leg: cut 2

cut for wing
glue line

glue line

glue line

turkey

bowl

Pilgrim house

Christmas Tree, Ornament, Snowman

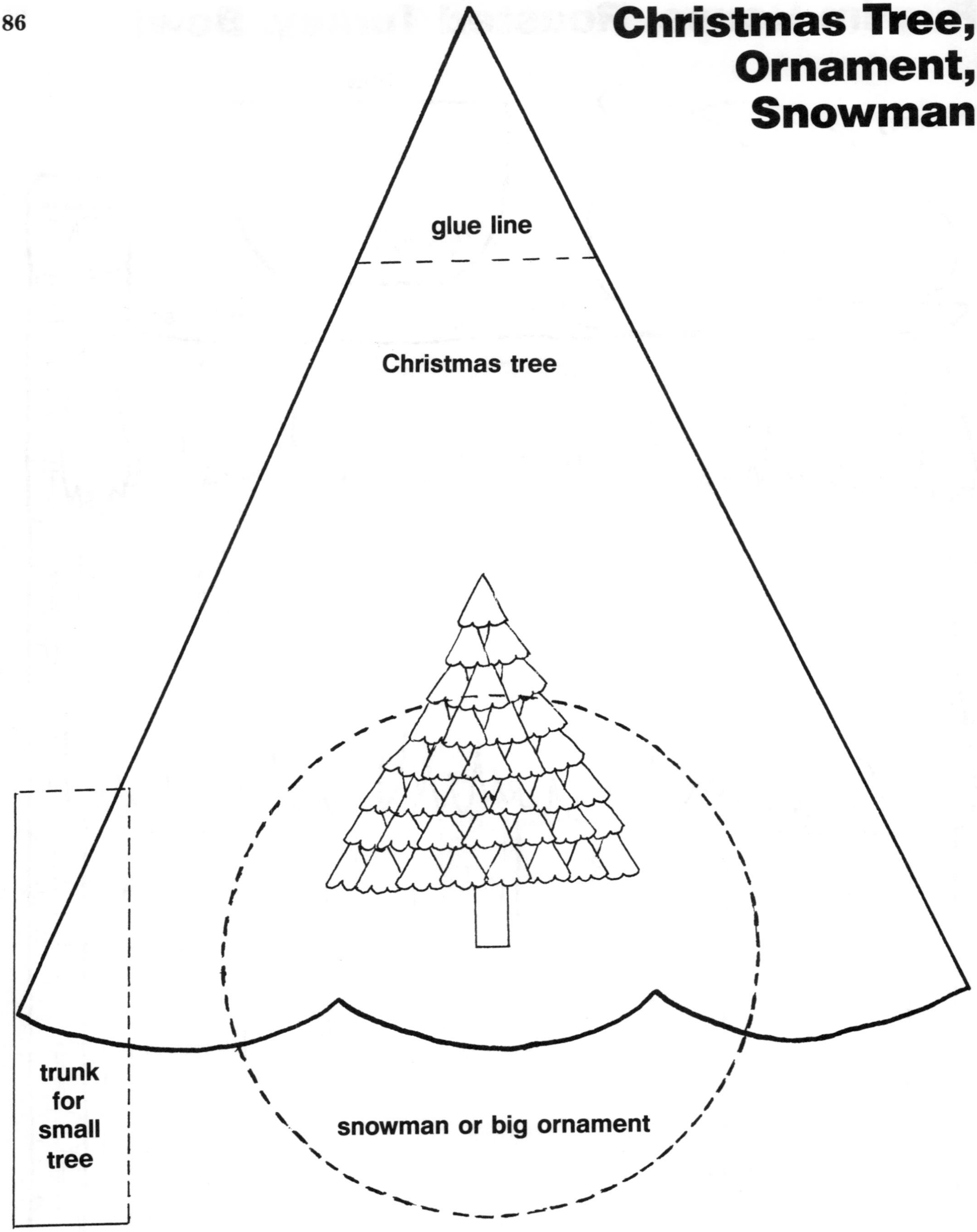

glue line

Christmas tree

trunk
for
small
tree

snowman or big ornament

Palm Tree, Stable, Star, Sheep, Manger, Baby Jesus, Walking Staff

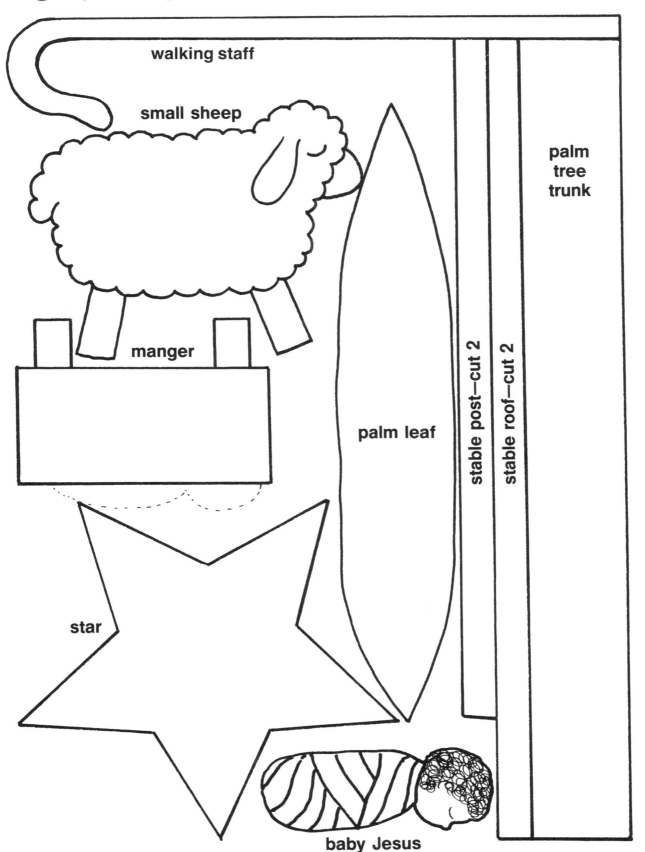

walking staff

small sheep

manger

palm leaf

stable post—cut 2

stable roof—cut 2

palm tree trunk

star

baby Jesus

Tablecloth, Bell, Face, Raindrop, Candy Cane, Menorah, Pancakes, Dreidel

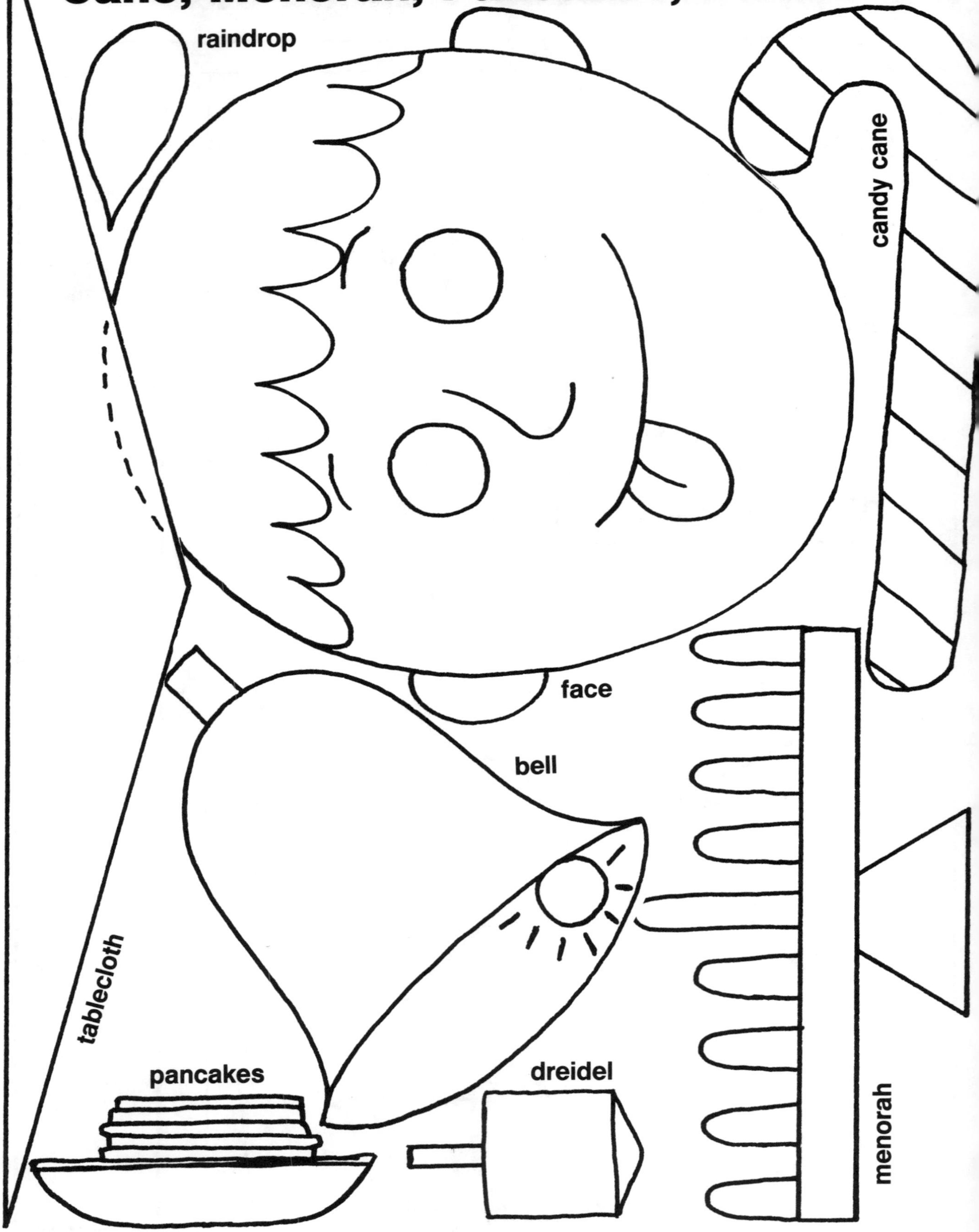

raindrop

candy cane

face

bell

tablecloth

pancakes

dreidel

menorah

Flag, Hand, Root, Cookie

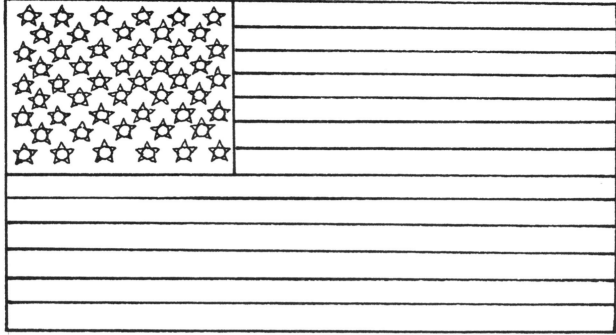

flag

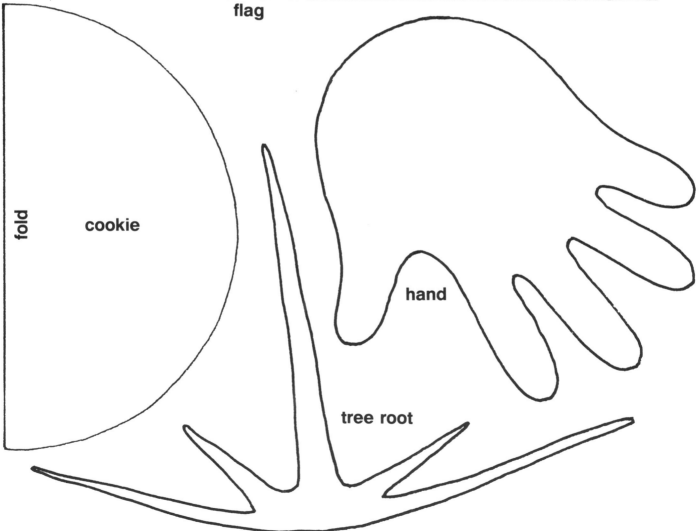

fold

cookie

hand

tree root

Rabbit, Sled, Bird, Bird Tracks, Snowflakes

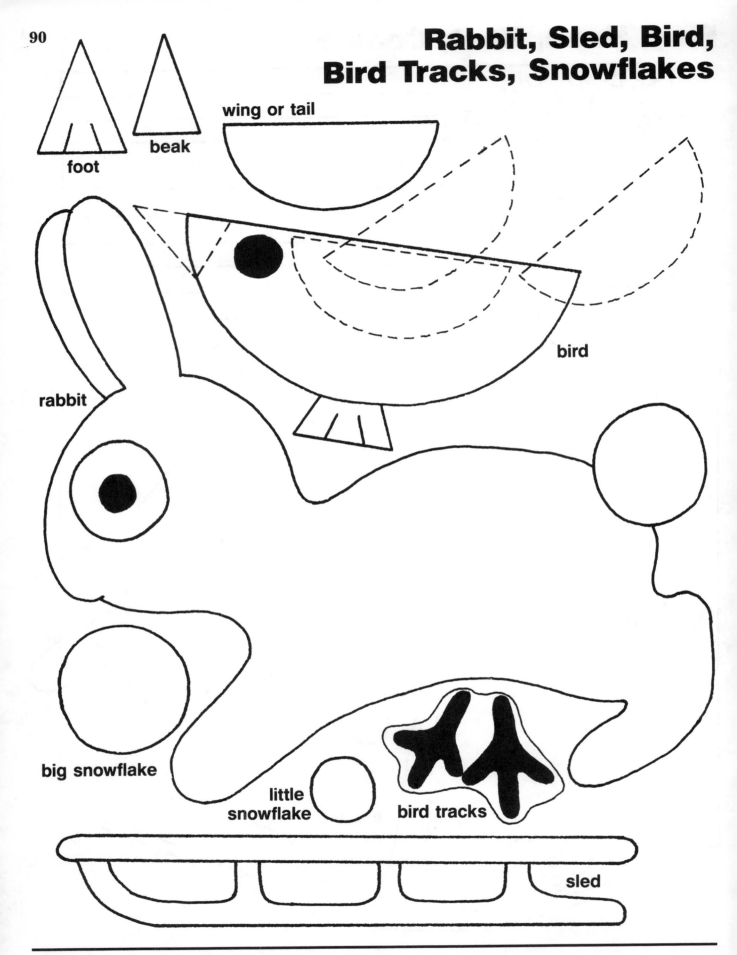

foot

beak

wing or tail

bird

rabbit

big snowflake

little snowflake

bird tracks

sled

Winter
Tree Trunk

big winter tree trunk—cut 7

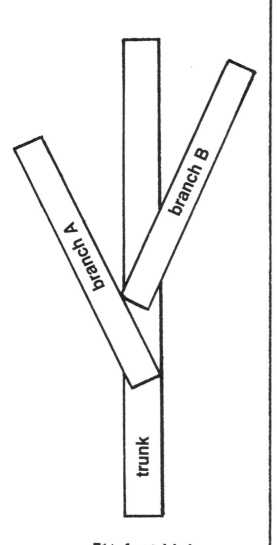

branch A

branch B

trunk

**5½ feet high
3-foot branches**

glue line

Winter Tree Branches, Pine Tree

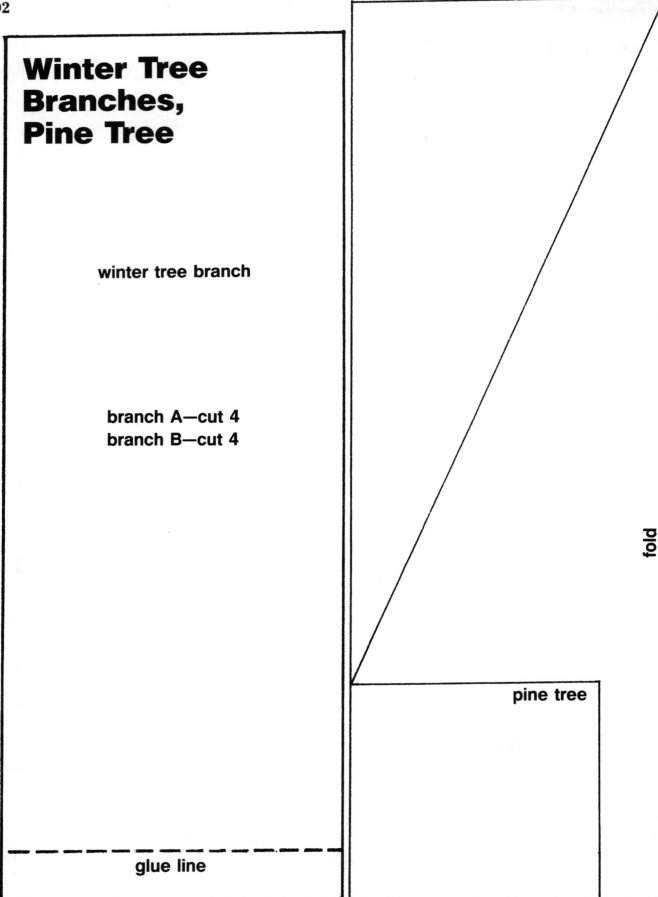

winter tree branch

branch A—cut 4
branch B—cut 4

glue line

fold

pine tree

cat

dog

Hearts, Turtles, Fish, Hamster

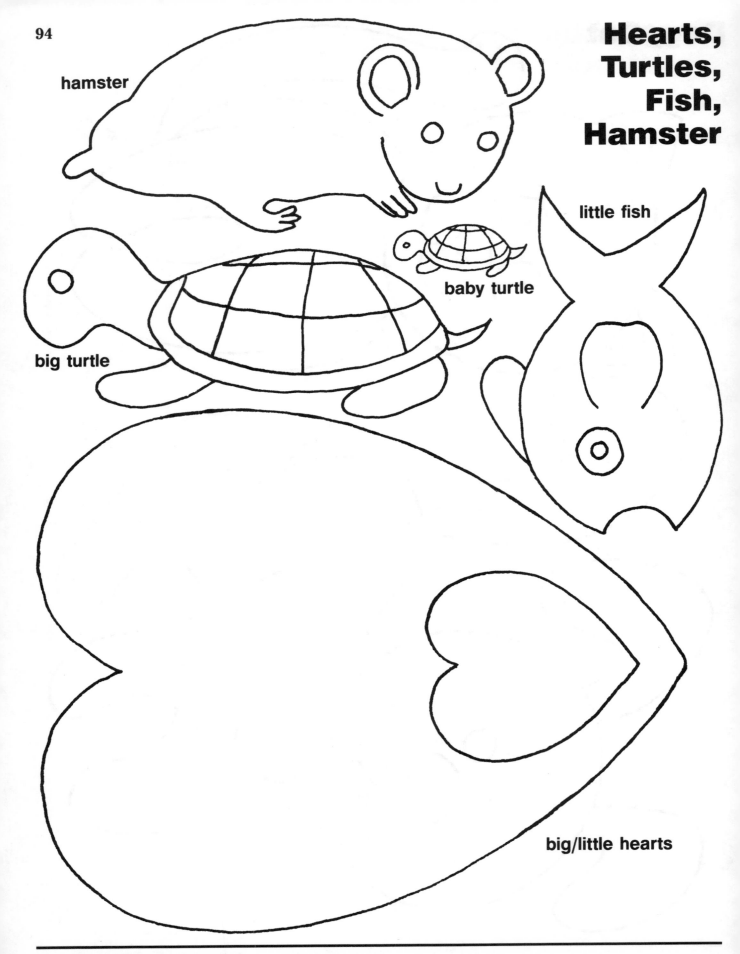

hamster

little fish

baby turtle

big turtle

big/little hearts

Face, Kite, Shamrock

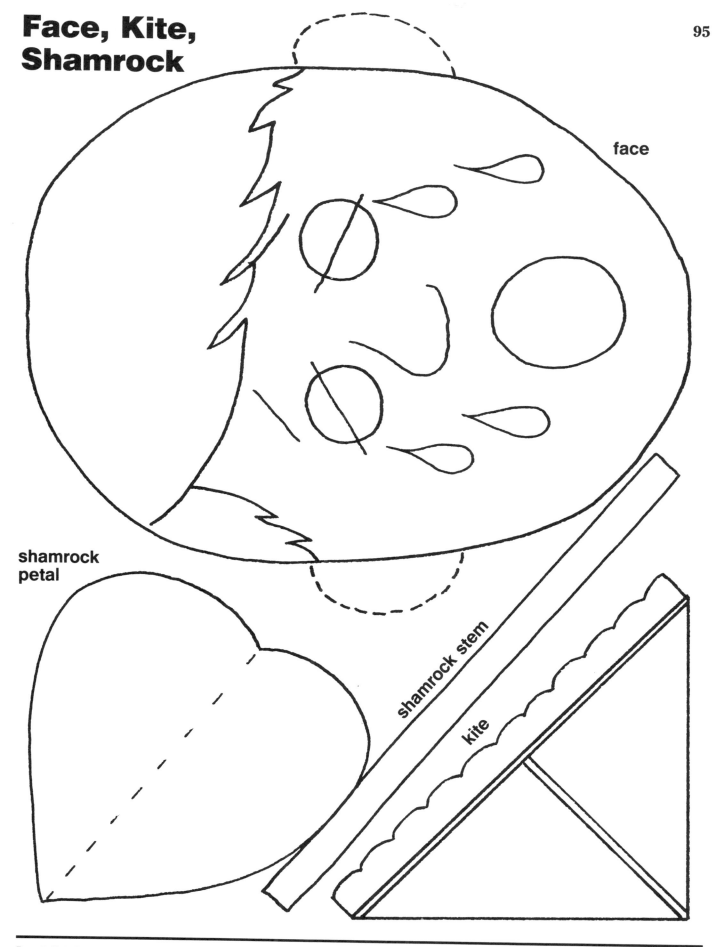

face

shamrock petal

shamrock stem

kite

From *Bulletin Boards for Every Month,* published by Scott, Foresman and Company.
Copyright © 1991 Jeanne Cheyney and Arnold Cheyney.

Bus, Hen, Red Cross Helmet, Ornament

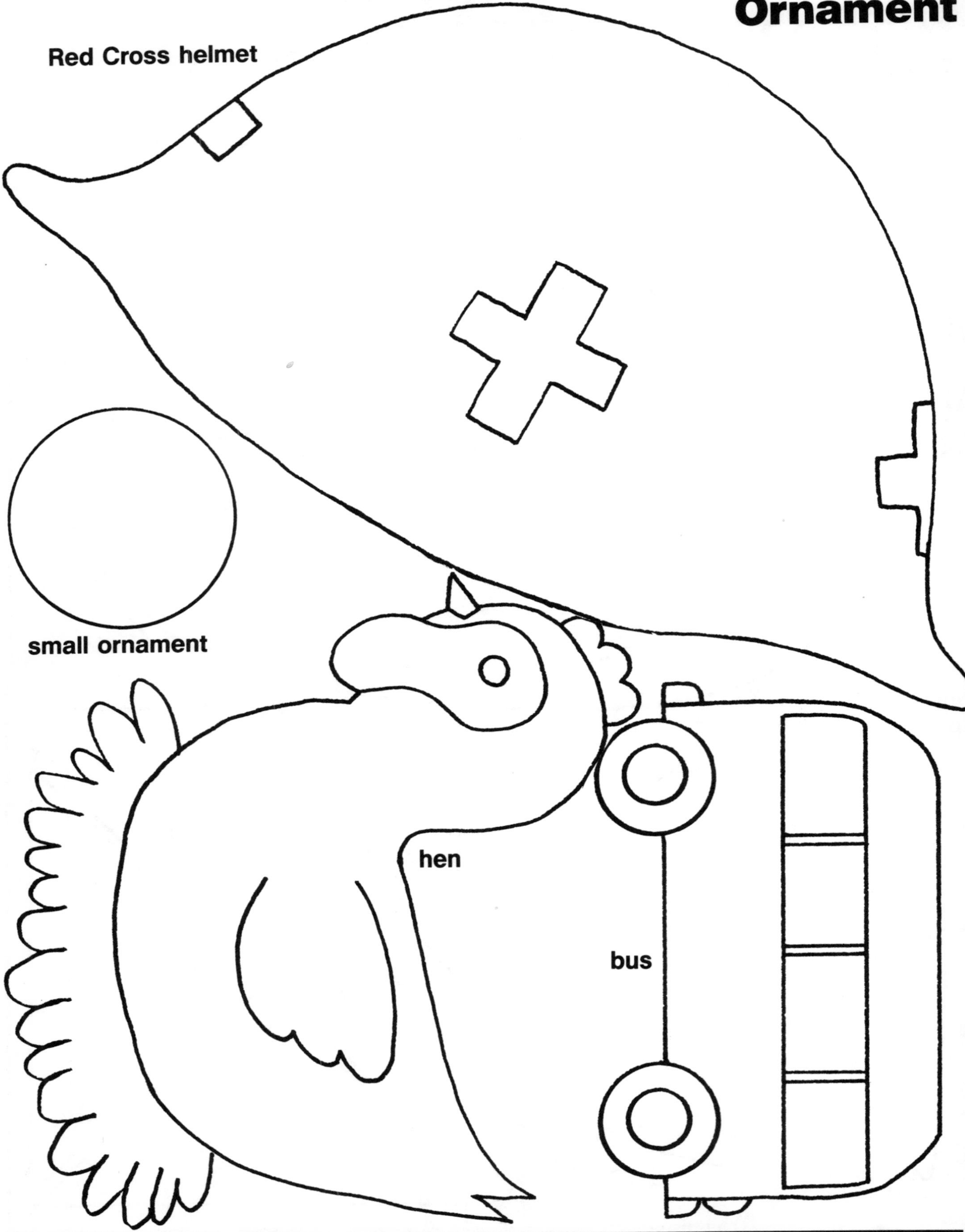

Red Cross helmet

small ornament

hen

bus

House,
Smoke,
Bird

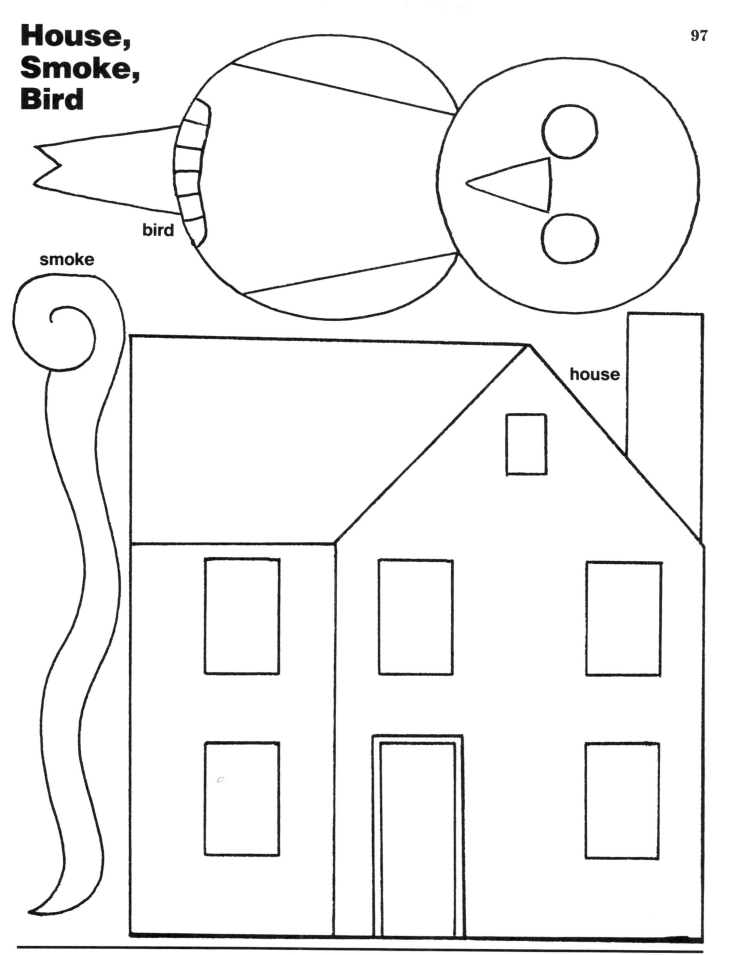

bird

smoke

house

Bears, Flower, Cloud, Puppy

bear
and cub

big
flower

cloud/puppy

Egg, Nest, Book, Matzos

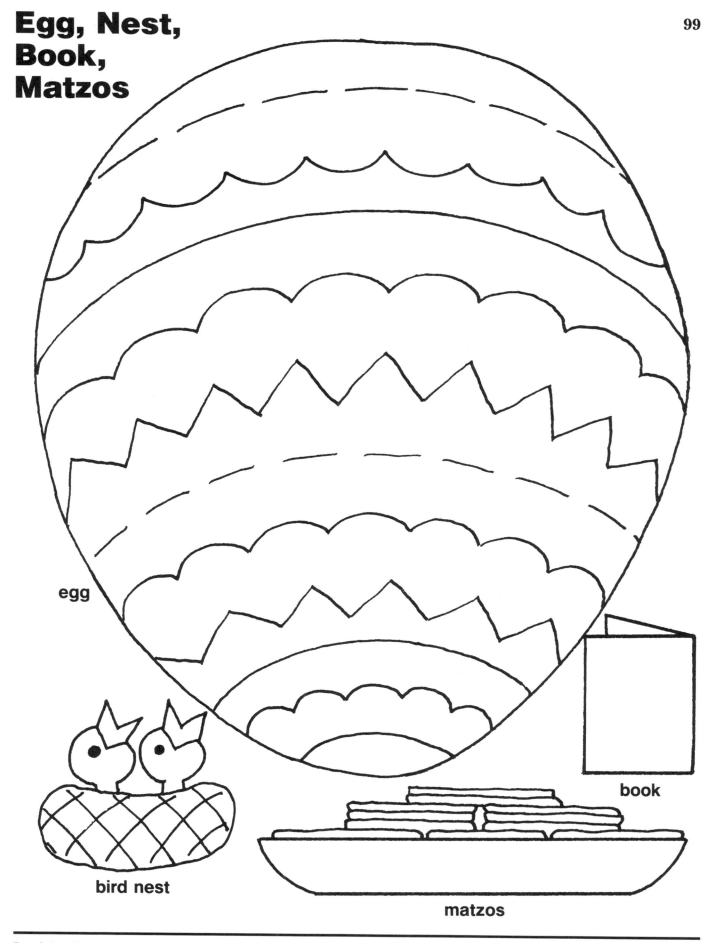

egg

bird nest

book

matzos

Sheep, Bunny Nest, Chicks, Flowers, Kitten

big sheep

chicks

bunny nest

little flower

kitten

flower

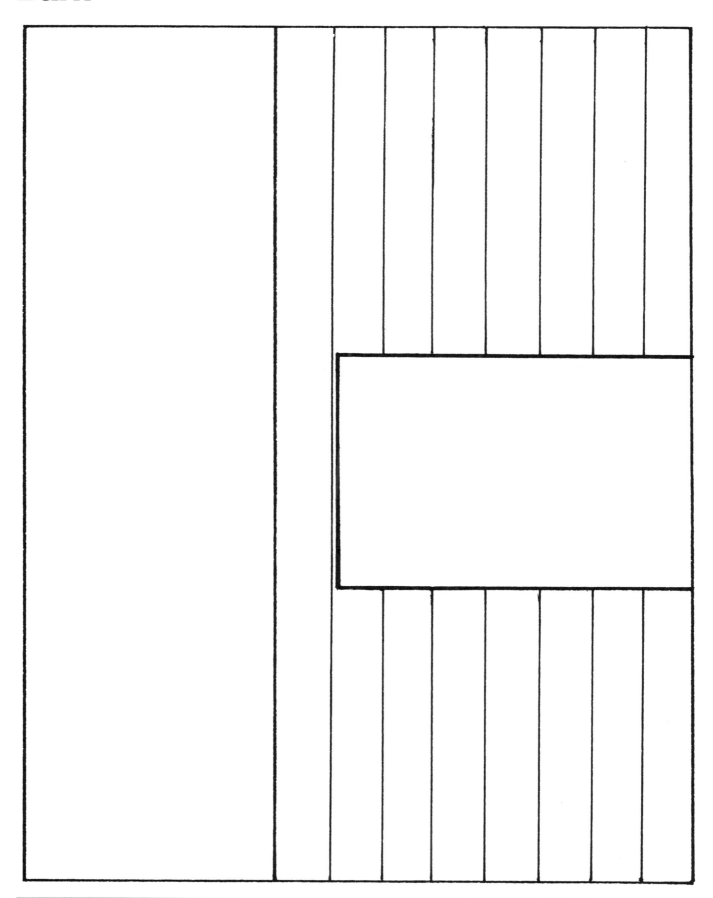

Flower, Pig, Picnic Jug, Sun

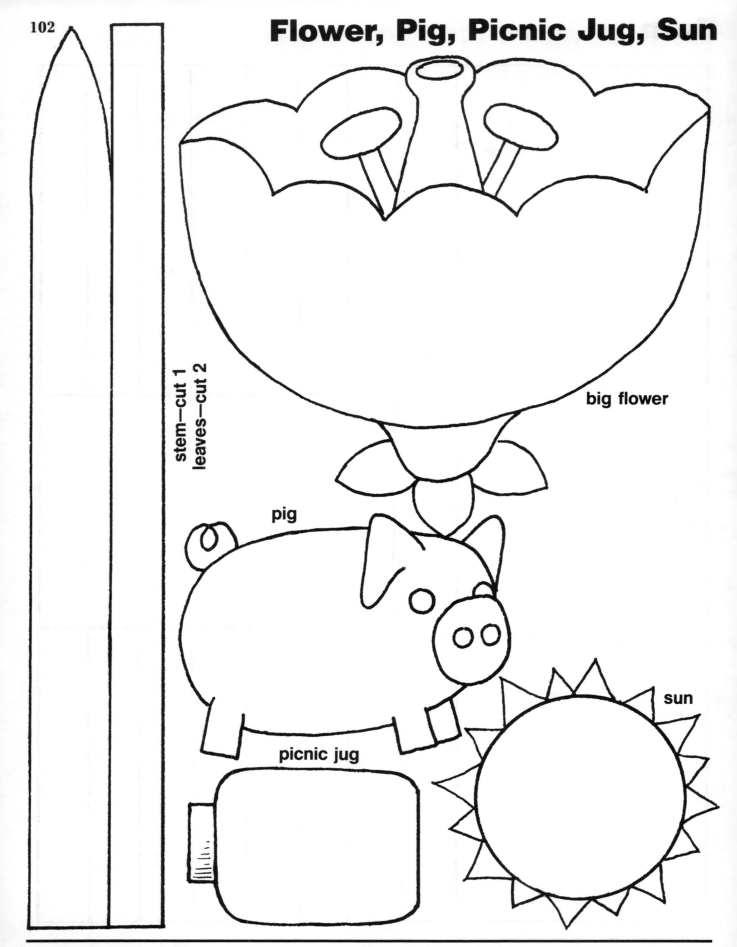

stem—cut 1
leaves—cut 2

big flower

pig

picnic jug

sun

Cow, Corn, Snake, Rabbit Tracks, Snowball

Cow, Corn, Snake, Rabbit Tracks, Snowball

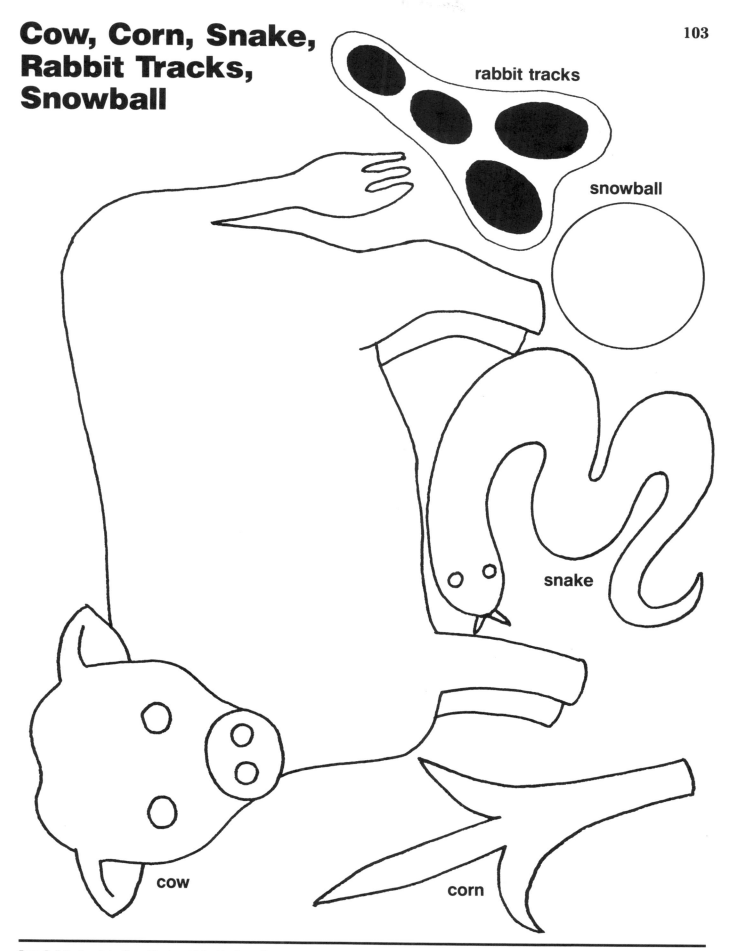

rabbit tracks

snowball

snake

cow

corn

Basketball, Hoop, Figures, Doll, Skateboard

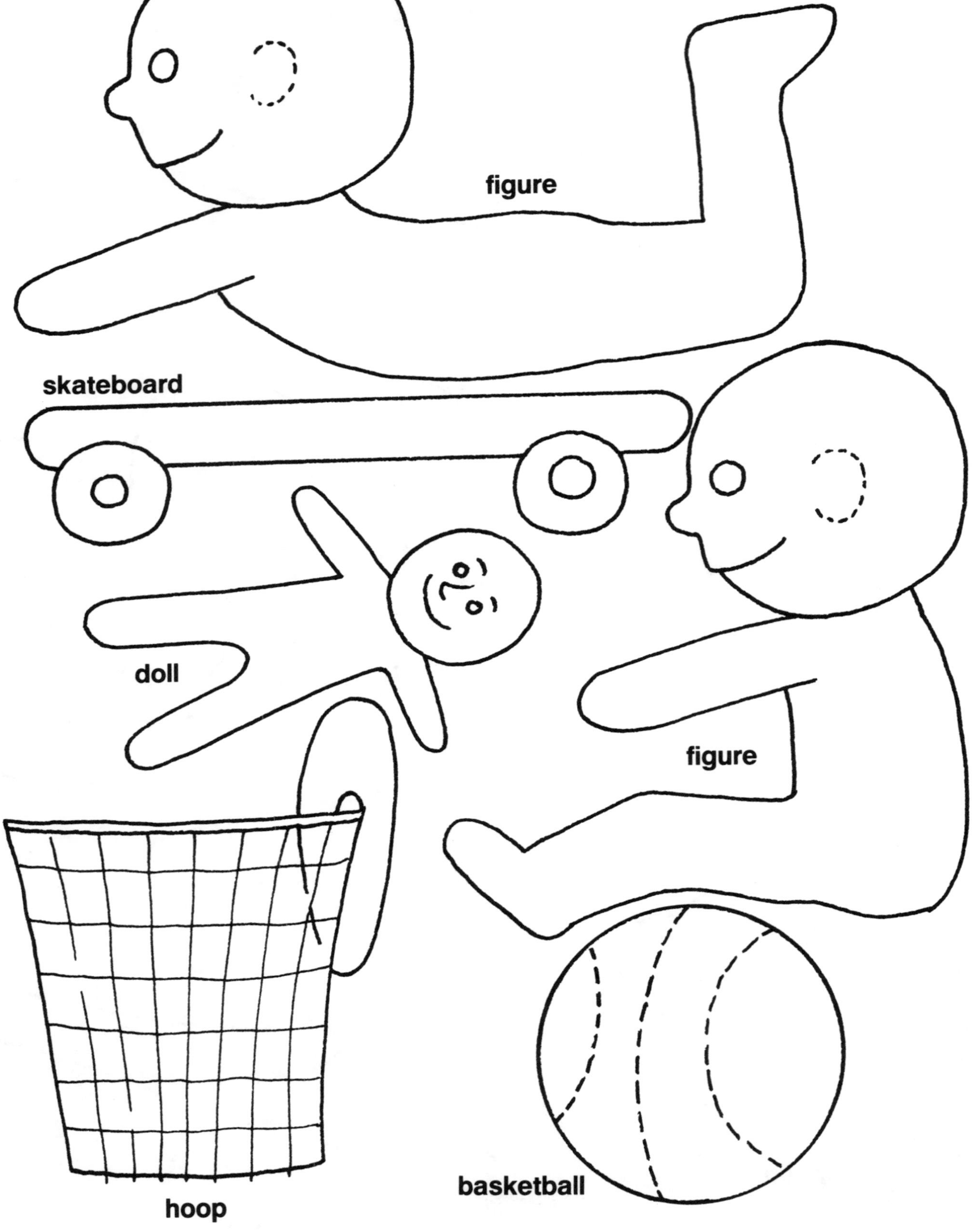

figure

skateboard

doll

figure

hoop

basketball

flames

logs

Face, Duck

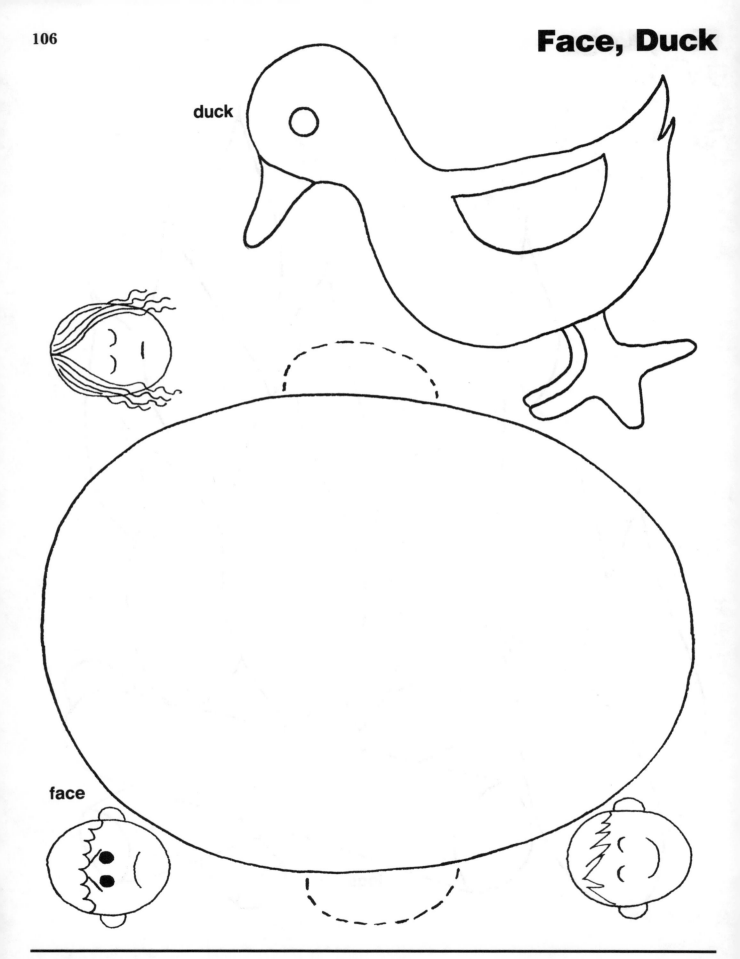

duck

face

Fireworks

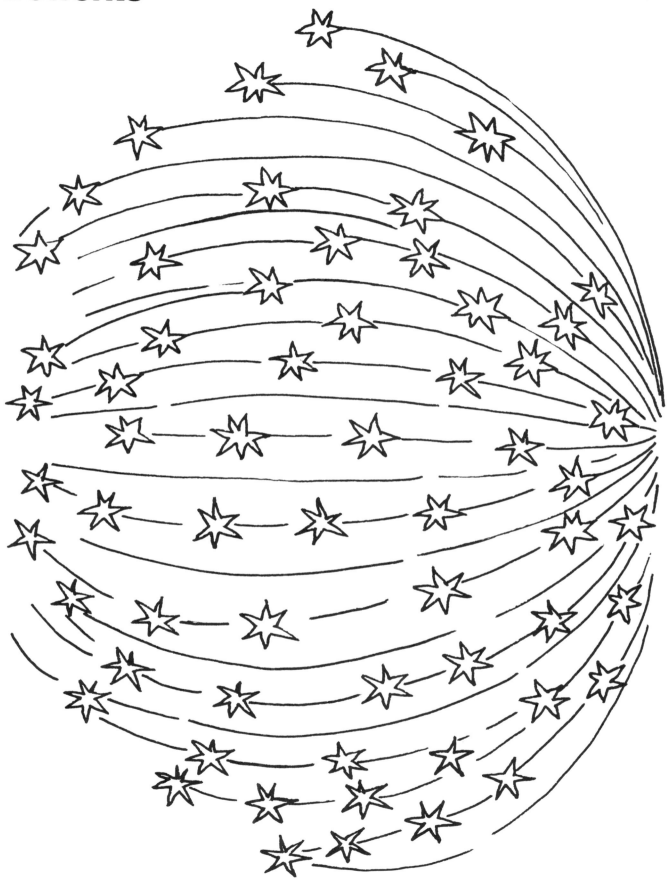

Uncle Sam

Hat, Flag, Instruments

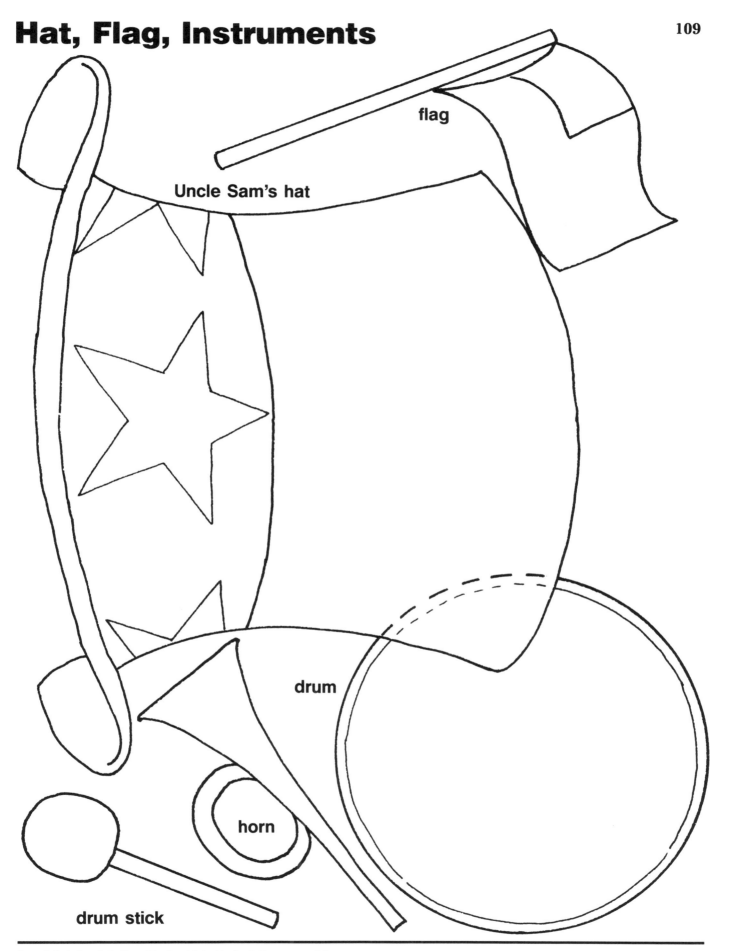

flag

Uncle Sam's hat

drum

horn

drum stick

Shells, Pail, Shovel, Figures, Ice Chest, Beach Ball

shovel

figure

pail

shell

shell

beach ball

shell

shell

shell

ice chest

shell

figure

Fish, Sailboat, Surfboard, Sandwiches

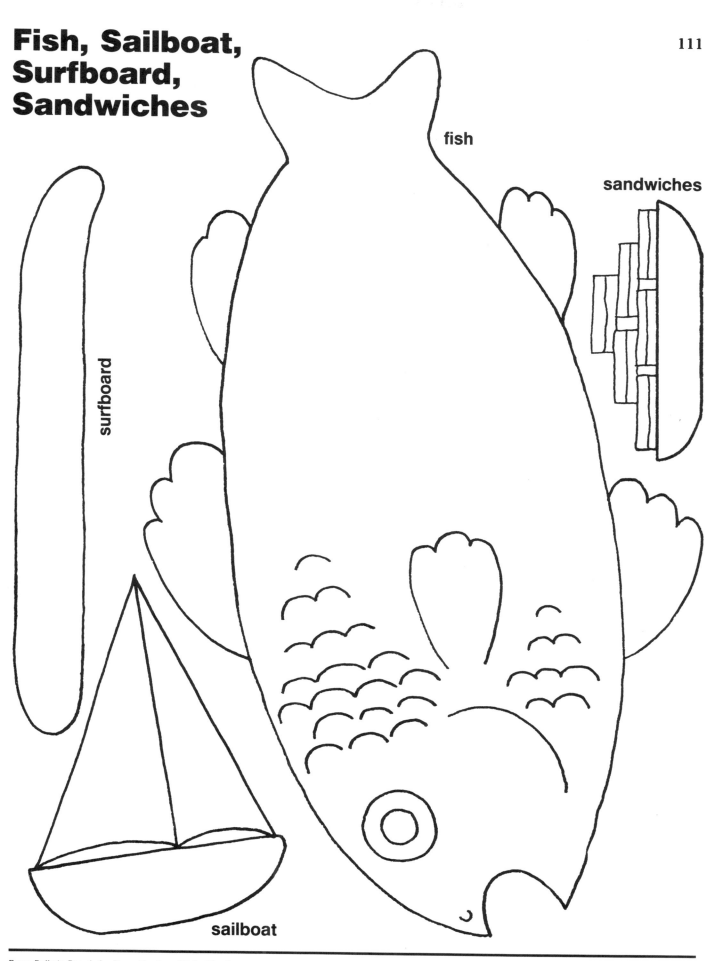

fish

sandwiches

surfboard

sailboat

From *Bulletin Boards for Every Month,* published by Scott, Foresman and Company.
Copyright © 1991 Jeanne Cheyney and Arnold Cheyney.

Waves,
Big Cloud,
Umbrella

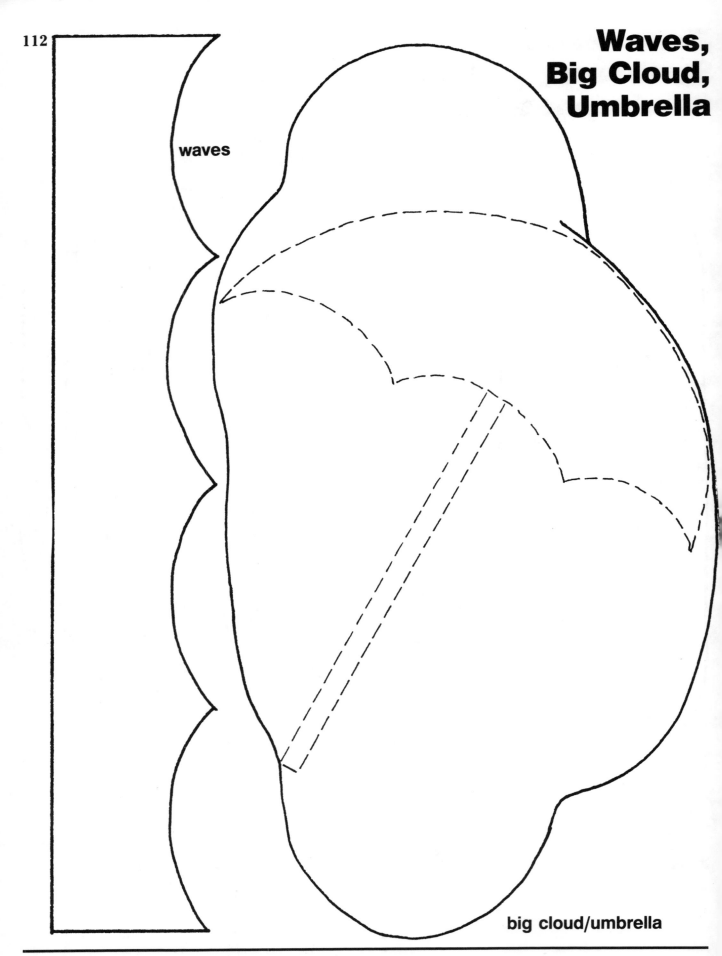

waves

big cloud/umbrella